FRANCIS FRITH'S

CANTERBURY - A HISTORY AND CELEBRATION

THE FRANCIS FRITH COLLECTION

www.francisfrith.com

CANTERBURY

A HISTORY AND CELEBRATION
OF THE CITY

MELODY RYALL

Produced by The Francis Frith Collection

www.francisfrith.com

First published in the United Kingdom in 2005
by The Francis Frith Collection®

Hardback Edition 2005 ISBN 1-84567-740-4
Paperback Edition 2011 ISBN 978-1-84589-619-5

British Library Cataloguing in Publication Data

Canterbury - A History and Celebration of the City
Melody Ryall

The Francis Frith Collection
Oakley Business Park, Wylye Road,
Dinton, Wiltshire SP3 5EU
Tel: +44 (0) 1722 716 376
Email: info@francisfrith.co.uk
www.francisfrith.com

Printed and bound in England

Front Cover: **CANTERBURY, MERCERY LANE c1952** C18027t

Additional modern photographs by Melody Ryall and Simon Hildrew.

Domesday extract used in timeline by kind permission of
Alecto Historical Editions, www.domesdaybook.org
Aerial photographs reproduced under licence from
Simmons Aerofilms Limited.
Historical Ordnance Survey maps reproduced under licence from Homecheck.co.uk

Every attempt has been made to contact copyright holders of
illustrative material. We will be happy to give full acknowledgement in future
editions for any items not credited. Any information should be directed to
The Francis Frith Collection.

*The colour-tinting in this book is for illustrative purposes only,
and is not intended to be historically accurate*

AS WITH ANY HISTORICAL DATABASE, THE FRANCIS FRITH ARCHIVE
IS CONSTANTLY BEING CORRECTED AND IMPROVED, AND THE
PUBLISHERS WOULD WELCOME INFORMATION ON OMISSIONS OR
INACCURACIES

Contents

CANTERBURY FROM THE AIR 1937 AFR3017

Historical Timeline for Canterbury

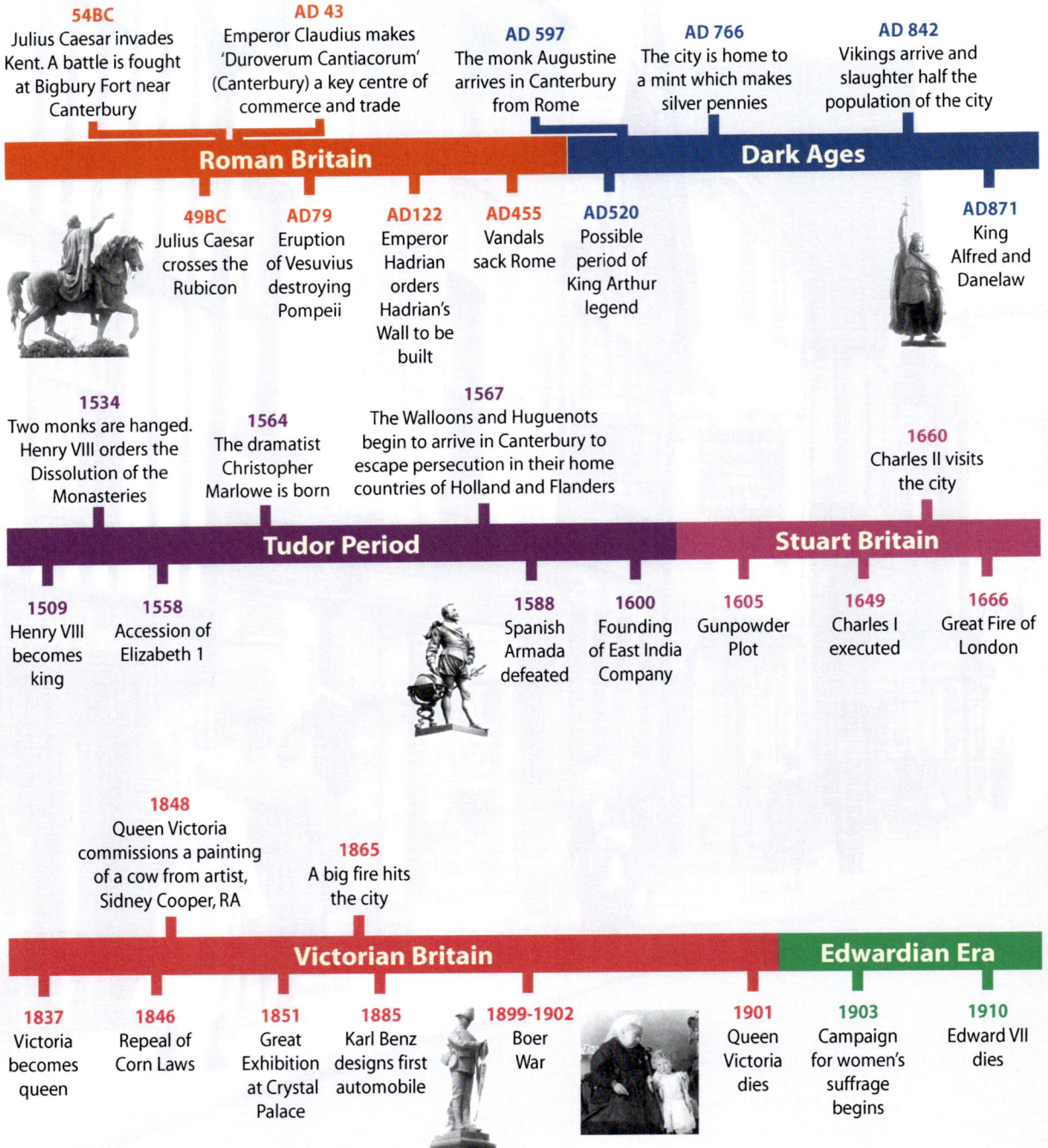

54BC
Julius Caesar invades Kent. A battle is fought at Bigbury Fort near Canterbury

AD 43
Emperor Claudius makes 'Duroverum Cantiacorum' (Canterbury) a key centre of commerce and trade

AD 597
The monk Augustine arrives in Canterbury from Rome

AD 766
The city is home to a mint which makes silver pennies

AD 842
Vikings arrive and slaughter half the population of the city

Roman Britain

Dark Ages

49BC
Julius Caesar crosses the Rubicon

AD79
Eruption of Vesuvius destroying Pompeii

AD122
Emperor Hadrian orders Hadrian's Wall to be built

AD455
Vandals sack Rome

AD520
Possible period of King Arthur legend

AD871
King Alfred and Danelaw

1534
Two monks are hanged. Henry VIII orders the Dissolution of the Monasteries

1564
The dramatist Christopher Marlowe is born

1567
The Walloons and Huguenots begin to arrive in Canterbury to escape persecution in their home countries of Holland and Flanders

1660
Charles II visits the city

Tudor Period

Stuart Britain

1509
Henry VIII becomes king

1558
Accession of Elizabeth 1

1588
Spanish Armada defeated

1600
Founding of East India Company

1605
Gunpowder Plot

1649
Charles I executed

1666
Great Fire of London

1848
Queen Victoria commissions a painting of a cow from artist, Sidney Cooper, RA

1865
A big fire hits the city

Victorian Britain

Edwardian Era

1837
Victoria becomes queen

1846
Repeal of Corn Laws

1851
Great Exhibition at Crystal Palace

1885
Karl Benz designs first automobile

1899-1902
Boer War

1901
Queen Victoria dies

1903
Campaign for women's suffrage begins

1910
Edward VII dies

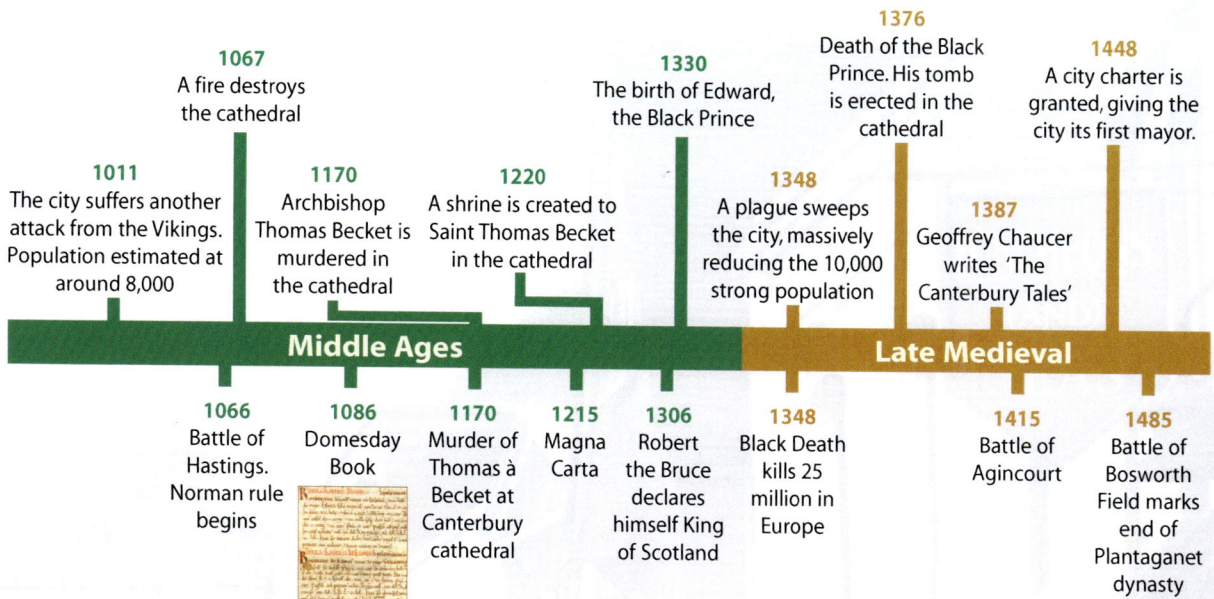

Middle Ages

1011
The city suffers another attack from the Vikings. Population estimated at around 8,000

1067
A fire destroys the cathedral

1170
Archbishop Thomas Becket is murdered in the cathedral

1220
A shrine is created to Saint Thomas Becket in the cathedral

1330
The birth of Edward, the Black Prince

1348
A plague sweeps the city, massively reducing the 10,000 strong population

1376
Death of the Black Prince. His tomb is erected in the cathedral

1387
Geoffrey Chaucer writes 'The Canterbury Tales'

1448
A city charter is granted, giving the city its first mayor.

Late Medieval

1066
Battle of Hastings. Norman rule begins

1086
Domesday Book

1170
Murder of Thomas à Becket at Canterbury cathedral

1215
Magna Carta

1306
Robert the Bruce declares himself King of Scotland

1348
Black Death kills 25 million in Europe

1415
Battle of Agincourt

1485
Battle of Bosworth Field marks end of Plantaganet dynasty

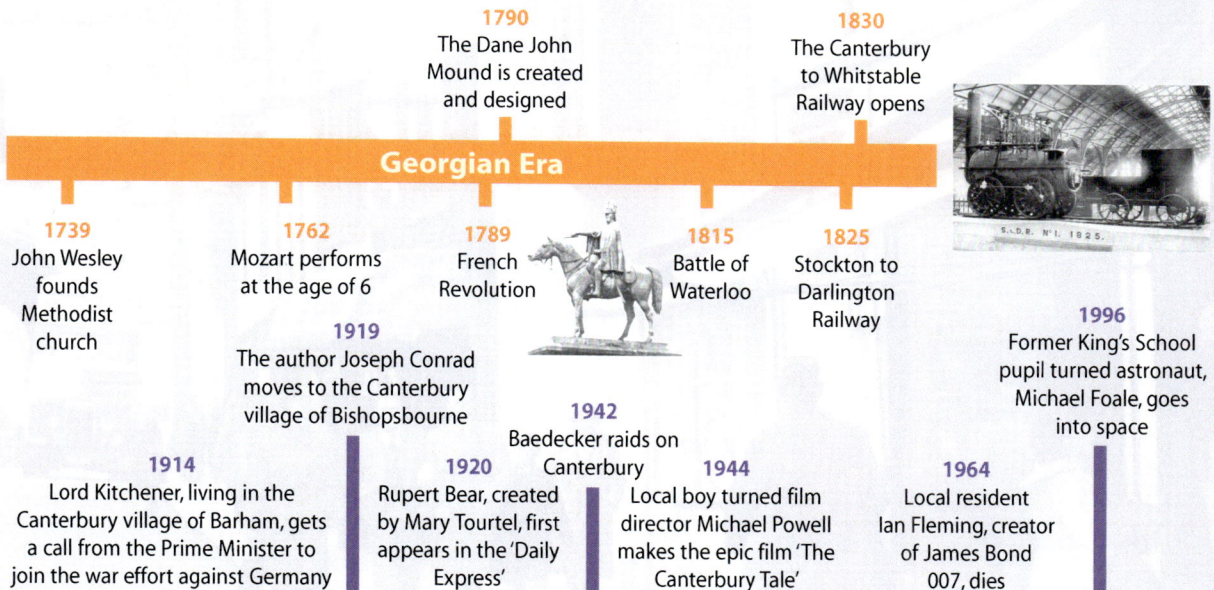

Georgian Era

1790
The Dane John Mound is created and designed

1830
The Canterbury to Whitstable Railway opens

1739
John Wesley founds Methodist church

1762
Mozart performs at the age of 6

1789
French Revolution

1815
Battle of Waterloo

1825
Stockton to Darlington Railway

1919
The author Joseph Conrad moves to the Canterbury village of Bishopsbourne

1996
Former King's School pupil turned astronaut, Michael Foale, goes into space

1914
Lord Kitchener, living in the Canterbury village of Barham, gets a call from the Prime Minister to join the war effort against Germany

1920
Rupert Bear, created by Mary Tourtel, first appears in the 'Daily Express'

1942
Baedecker raids on Canterbury

1944
Local boy turned film director Michael Powell makes the epic film 'The Canterbury Tale'

1964
Local resident Ian Fleming, creator of James Bond 007, dies

20th Century Britain

1914
First World War begins

1926
John Logie Baird obtains first television picture

1939
Outbreak of Second World War

1956
Suez Crisis

1966
England win World Cup

1969
First man on the Moon

1982
Falklands Conflict

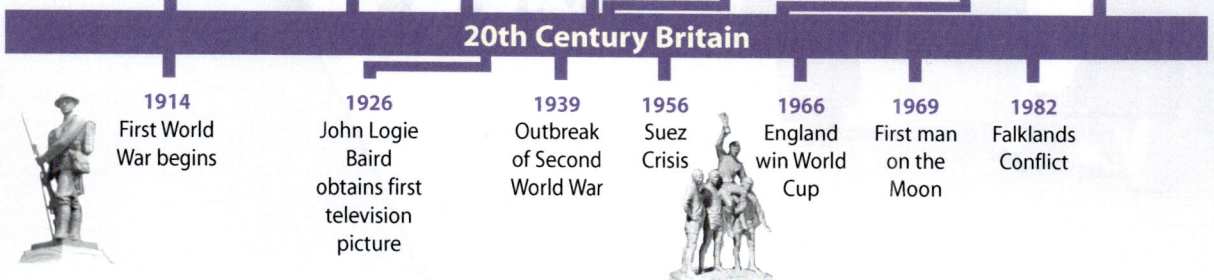

CANTERBURY

Introduction

THE CATHEDRAL FROM THE AIR c1935 C18061

'EVERYBODY'S heard of Canterbury!' exclaims one of the characters in Michael Powell's and Emeric Pressburger's 1944 film classic, 'The Canterbury Tale'.

And of course most of us, somehow and somewhere, know the story of the medieval pilgrims who set out on their long journey to reach the city that offered all visitors either blessings or a penance.

But just why this ancient city with its Roman roots is so famous and so dominant in our knowledge of British history is a question many scholars over the years have sought to answer, including the admirable 20th century city archivist Dr William Urry. His work has proved a constant resource for many interested in the life and times of the city.

But while many guidebooks about Canterbury exist, it is difficult, according to some modern-day academics, to find a precise all-encompassing history book of this fascinating place.

Is it then because there is so very much to Canterbury? For a start, it is home to one of the world's most famous cathedrals, its King's School is the oldest public school in Britain, it has medieval streets, mysterious narrow alleyways, Norman churches and Roman ruins. It was the scene of the brutal slaying of the Archbishop, Thomas Becket, in the 12th century, and it was the birthplace of the Elizabethan playwright, Christopher Marlowe - the man who some believe contributed more to the canon of English literature than William Shakespeare. We must not forget too the indefatigable Geoffrey Chaucer, whose medieval tales brought literary fame and fortune to the city, or the artist Sidney Cooper, who is still remembered today with a High Street gallery and an exhibition hall named after him near the Marlowe Theatre in the Friars area of the city.

Victorian days heralded a visit by Charles Dickens too. In St Dunstan's Street a plaque sits above the door of the Dickens Inn which notes the author describing the property as the home of Agnes Wickfield - the daughter of the solicitor in his novel, 'David Copperfield'.

In the 20th century Canterbury was home to Mary Tourtel, the creator of the children's storybook character Rupert Bear. Nearby in the seaside town of Whitstable lives Oliver Postgate who created the children's favourite, Bagpuss. The Hammer Horror film star and actor Peter Cushing also lived in Whitstable until his death in 1994. The jazz hero Chris Barber is also a 20th century Canterbury lad, and 1977 saw the birth in the city of the Hollywood star Orlando Bloom, the actor who shot to fame as Legolas in the award winning film trilogy, 'Lord of the Rings'.

In 1964 the city's University of Kent was built, and along with Christ Church College has proved to be the alma mater of many of today's movers and shakers.

It cannot be denied that Canterbury boasts a rich unshakeable charm, with foundations and history that continue to outshine each new generation of cultural and socio-economic change that comes its way.

But where exactly is the city on the world map? Canterbury is built on a site that for more than 2000 years has provided an arena for a multitude of important events in British history. The city is situated in the east of Kent and lies in the valley of the River Stour. When we look south we can see the North Downs and the coast is north and east. Across the English Channel at Dover sits mainland Europe, which is just 20 miles away.

What is well worth noting though as we embark on our pilgrimage through the life and characters of the city is the remarkable timing of the Powell and Pressburger film. For, as the actors played out their scenes in this compelling wartime drama that was based on Chaucer's 14th-century tales, audiences then and now were able to see, on film, the bombed-out streets of the city. Palace Street and the High Street are shown, half in ruins, and also the remains of the noble St George's Church, which is now just a clock-tower, but nevertheless is still standing proud today with a face full of Roman numerals at the top end of George Street.

Among all this devastation on view in 1944, however, lay a wealth of history just begging to be uncovered. Hitler's bombs may well have ripped apart the Canterbury of the 1940s but they had also exposed for the first time in hundreds of years the very foundations of Roman life.

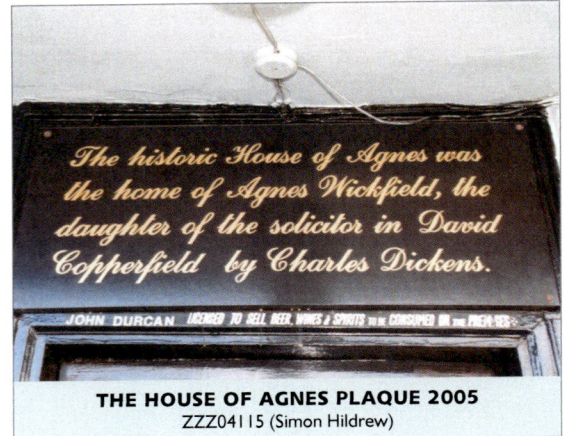

THE HOUSE OF AGNES PLAQUE 2005
ZZZ04115 (Simon Hildrew)

The famous plaque above the Dickens Inn in St Dunstan's Street

THE HOUSE OF AGNES 2005 C18701k (Simon Hildrew)

CHAPTER ONE

Togas, Tyrannies and the Foundations of Greatness

This reconstruction view of Roman Canterbury in about AD 300 is an artist's view by Ivan Lapper, based on expert archaeological research. The giant theatre at the bottom of St Margaret's Street, built to seat 3,000 people, can be seen in the centre of the picture.

BY THE MIDDLE of the 20th century archaeologists knew that Canterbury had once been a marshland area, before Bronze and Iron Age families cultivated it, made fortified villages, and fought to shield it from invasions from across the Channel.

Indeed at the corner of St John's Lane and Castle Street historians discovered traces of a residential area dating back to about 300 BC. In 1946 a typical prehistoric gully was unearthed on the south side of St George's Street and it was here that a vast quantity of pottery was found, dating from around AD 10-40.

When the tribes known as the Belgae dominated the east Kent landscape, Prince Vodenos was a ruler. This was proved by the discovery of a silver coin bearing his profile, also in St Margaret's Street, on the site of the old Marlowe Theatre (now demolished).

Did you know?

It was the Belgae, who lived at a large Iron Age fort at Bigbury, four kilometres west of modern Canterbury, who named the area 'Durovernum' (fort by the alder swamp). This tribe were among the first ever recorded to be living in the area.

A RECONSTRUCTION OF AN IRON AGE ROUNDHOUSE
ZZZ01297 (Reproduced by kind permission of the
Ancient Technology Centre, Cranborne, Dorset)

So centuries later when the bombs had exploded in the streets during the Second World War, hundreds of ancient foundations provided vital historical information. Although the damage to the city was dreadful, one benefit to archaeologists and historians was that so much of the buried past was exposed for them to study.

A Canterbury Excavation Committee was formed, and Mrs Audrey Williams and Mr Sheppard Frere, both Fellows of the Society of Archaeologists, started the first serious digs in the city. Much of the work enabled these two dedicated archaeologists to attempt to figure out a Roman street plan of the unusual city that had grown up at the bottom of the Stour Valley. Because the river runs through the area the Romans would not have designated the site for a military camp. It was to be primarily a residential town boasting typical Roman centres of community activity.

In the fourth edition of Mr Frere's summary of Roman Canterbury (available at the Roman Museum) he states that the city was spread out on both sides of an important ford across the River Stour. This ford was part of Watling Street, one of three Roman roads which met at the point where the new city lay. Basing a new town or city in a valley near a river was typical of Roman planners and engineers. They aimed to set out a series of key buildings like a chessboard in an area.

So when exactly did the area encounter the Romans? Julius Caesar had arrived near Deal on the coast of Kent in 55 BC, bringing more than 10,000 soldiers with him. His arrival did not go unopposed as Belgic tribesmen lay in wait to attack. A battle raged for several days until the Belgae asked for peace.

In Caesar's commentaries on the Gallic Wars, written about 55 BC, he wrote: 'And now, as our soldiers were hesitating, mostly because of the depth of the water, the man who carried the eagle of the Tenth Legion, after praying to the gods that his act would bring good luck to the legion, shouted out loudly, "Jump down, men, unless you want to betray your eagle to the enemy. I at any rate shall have done my duty to my country and general." With these words he flung himself from the ship and began to carry the eagle towards the enemy. Then the soldiers jumped down from the ship all together, urging each other not to allow a disgrace like that to happen.'

Records show that Julius Caesar and his legions stormed into the thriving little settlements in the area we now call Canterbury

GENERAL VIEW c1953 C18003

a year later, in 54 BC. It is believed a battle took place at nearby Bigbury Fort at this time. However, when Caesar and his forces arrived in Canterbury he was not ungenerous to its peoples, even though he received a hostile welcome on the Kent coast.

According to ancient records Caesar described the locals as 'quite civilised' and in his commentaries on the Gallic Wars he described the same people of Kent as wearing their hair long and living on milk and meat and sporting animal skins to cover their flesh.

What he meant by 'civilised' is interesting. He was obviously impressed that not all ancient Britons were complete savages or utter barbarians as his peers in Rome 2,000 kilometres away would describe the people who lived in the land they called Britannia! However, this peculiar affection for the local Belgae did not persuade him to stay long. After Caesar returned to Italy the longhaired, animal-skin-wearing community in this area of east Kent was left to fend for itself for almost another 100 years.

MERCERY LANE c1952 C18027

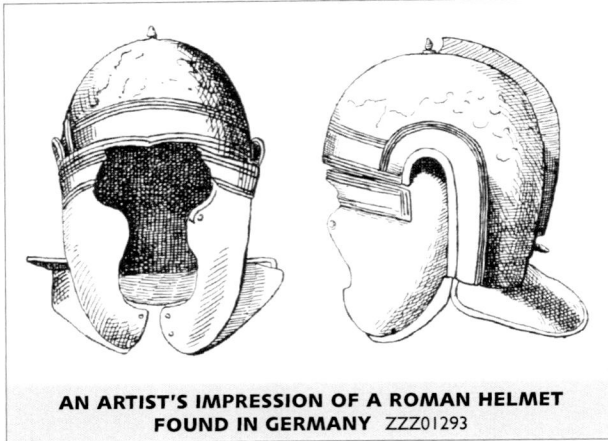

AN ARTIST'S IMPRESSION OF A ROMAN HELMET FOUND IN GERMANY ZZZ01293

In AD 43 the Romans, this time led by the Emperor Claudius, returned in earnest and 'Duovernum Cantiacorum' (Canterbury) became an important capital, linking trading ports to London. The humble native people, who once reared sheep, milked cattle and planted crops for a living, were now wearing togas, visiting theatres to see the plays of Plautus and Terence, enjoying baths, experiencing the beauty of mosaic flooring and visiting sacred temples. The Romans named the locals the Cantiaci and the city became the capital of Kent.

If residents played it clever they could also enjoy the new lifestyles offered them by their Roman conquerors. They could contribute to debates at the newly built forum and civic centre, learn a host of new crafts, worship new gods like Mars or Jupiter. They married Romans, bore their children, and created new generations with Roman blood coursing through their veins. However, not everyone loved the conquerors with their red wine, lofty chat, togas and sophisticated ways. In

1977 historians digging in the city found a deep pit containing two skeletons of Roman soldiers with their swords by their sides. Historians believe they had been murdered.

Usually in old Durovernum the dead were buried outside the city in large cemeteries. Such ancient burial grounds have been discovered over the years in Wincheap, Dane John Gardens and the north-west side of St Dunstan's. Excavations reveal the only exception to this steadfast Roman rule - babies and children were buried inside the city. Their skeletons have been discovered in

DANE JOHN GARDENS 1921 70333

St Margaret's Street and Butchery Lane.

Today, vital evidence of the city's Roman period can still be seen. The original stone in Westgate towers is of Roman origin, according to the archaeologist Sheppard Frere, and the foundations of the walls to the city and ancient trenches became evident after various excavations in Dane John Gardens and Burgate in the middle of the last century. In the Middle Ages however, the walls we now see were built with Kentish flint.

To get a true flavour of life back in the times of Roman Canterbury it is important to visit the city's Roman Museum, in a narrow lane known as the Longmarket. Inside this grand building with its pillared frontage and mosaic front step there are a host of amazing artefacts which give the inhabitants of the 21st century a superb insight into those ancient times.

Here it is possible to see a wealth of information about Roman Canterbury. There is a gallery of fascinating archaeological finds, which include jewellery, cooking utensils, pottery, ornaments, weapons and even hairpins. There is also a touch-screen computer game. Remains of a Roman

house, showing mosaic floors, are also on view at the museum plus an impressive computer program with clever reconstructions and a screen tour of a Roman house site. In this new millennium the friendly staff at the city's Roman Museum are introducing us to more of the fabric of the city and the foundations upon which so much has grown and evolved over the last 2000 years.

The museum reveals how, since 1945, redevelopment in the city has provided some lucky breaks for archaeologists. The discovery of mosaic pavements in Butchery Lane and ancient baths and theatre foundations in St Margaret's Street are among many amazing reminders of Canterbury's Roman history and the people who lived there.

TILES AT THE ROMAN BATHS IN ST MARGARET'S STREET 2005 C18702k (Simon Hildrew)

Pillars of ancient tiles were used to support the floors of the bath-house, so that warm air could circulate as part of the Roman hypocaust system of under-floor central heating. Today these are on show on the ground floor of Waterstone's bookshop in St Margaret's Street.

CANTERBURY ROMAN MUSEUM

AN ARCHAEOLOGICAL QUEST FOR THE BURIED ROMAN TOWN
CANTERBURY ROMAN MUSEUM

ROMAN MUSEUM LEAFLET ZZZ04118
(© Canterbury Museums, copyright reserved 2005.
Reproduced by permission of the senior curator, Ken Reedie)

We learn how in the last 60 years archaeologists have dug deep to discover a matrix of roads created from impacted gravel and bordered with timber drains. These Roman roads formed an irregularly shaped city that boasted baths, temples, a theatre and a forum. Exotic discoveries include ancient marble statues and edifices, all work created by foreign craftsmen brought into the city by the Romans during their rule.

The Roman Museum was opened in 1972 then the remains were covered over until 1989 when the whole site was redeveloped. It reopened again in 1994, and attracts thousands of visitors every year.

The Roman Museum's own Bill Herbert is happy to show visitors a fine collection of glass, including a 2nd century vase which was found near Bourne Park lake at the neighbouring village of Bishopsbourne.

Bill says: 'This vase we know was made in Cologne, which proves the Romans imported many everyday items to Canterbury. Among the most popular artefacts we have are two Roman cavalry swords. These are about the only two of their kind in Britain and are very unusual. These were discovered near the old gasworks.'

According to Bill and other local historians, the Romans chose to centre themselves in Canterbury because the Cantiaci had made such an impact on the area with early settlements and land developments.

Bill explains: 'During the Roman times in Canterbury, there was a population of 6,000-10,000. We know that the theatre situated at the southern end of St Margaret's Street

> ## Did you know?
> Among the most famous treasures on show at the Roman Museum is an ancient and remarkable collection of silver spoons. These were discovered in 1962, by workmen digging up the roundabout at Rheims Way near the old tannery. In 2003 television presenter Lisa Tarbuck visited the museum as part of the Channel Four programme 'The Big Dig'.

had seating room for 3,000, and was one of the largest Roman theatres ever discovered in Britain. Not only would audiences see plays with actors wearing huge masks, but they would also go there in those times for important religious festivals.'

It is the evidence of this Roman theatre that provides us with so much information about the wealth that existed in the city at the time. The size and scale of the theatre was regarded as monumental. It played a huge role in filtering the message of Roman culture and idealism through to the audiences who sat in awe of its majestic and dramatic performances.

In the 19th century two halves of a large altar were discovered in Mercery Lane, and evidence of a large Roman building was discovered in 1867 by the city engineer, Mr Pillborrow, in Sun Street and Guildhall Street.

However, for many archaeologists specialising in the Roman era today there are frustrations. One of the last great discoveries to be made in the city would be the forum, but like many sites rich in history there are listed buildings constructed on the top of the remains.

THE THREE TUNS PUB, SITE OF
THE ROMAN THEATRE 2005   C18703k (Simon Hildrew)

Beneath the Three Tuns pub in St Margaret's Street lie the remains of the massive Roman theatre.

MERCERY LANE c1952   C18027

Bill says: 'We think the forum is probably underneath the County Hotel in the High Street, and we believe there must be some amazing Roman ruins underneath what is now Clark's shoe shop nearby, but these are wonderful medieval buildings and there is no way we can excavate around them.'

Archaeologists are certain Canterbury also had a temple that would probably be found in the area of Beercart Lane, and that there is very likely to be evidence of a Roman temple under the cathedral too, but as Bill Herbert says, there is not much chance of archaeologists digging about in the cathedral foundations in the near future.

Archaeologists also believe a civic centre is buried in the centre of the city, but to reach the Roman ruins experts must go down about seven feet. Today, many historians would like to excavate the site of the old tannery but this would prove a tremendously expensive experience because the ground is contaminated.

What we do know, though, is that buildings back in the 'Durovernum Cantiacorum' of AD 70 would have been mostly single storey with timber frames and foundations of flint. Roofs were probably tiled. Wealthy Romans had houses with central heating and beautiful mosaic floors; in 1758 a mosaic path in good condition was unearthed on the site of the County Hotel and another one was discovered in Burgate Street in 1868.

In AD 313 the Roman emperor Constantine recognised Christianity as the official religion in the empire. Christians could openly practise their own faith. In the early 8th century the Anglo-Saxon monk Bede wrote the 'Ecclesiastical History of the English Nation'. In this book he recorded how, during the Roman occupation, a church was built in honour of St Martin on the east side of what is now Canterbury. This old church stood where North Holmes Road now runs.

However, a few hundred years before Bede made this statement, the city had come under attack from raiders from across the North Sea, along with other areas in east Kent, including Richborough, Reculver, Dover and Lympne. Forts were built in these towns, but all that is left today of Canterbury's Roman walls are

Did you know?

The skeletons of a Romano-British family were unearthed by city archaeologist Paul Bennett during a dig near Stour Street in the 1980s. The family of four had been brutally murdered and hastily buried, but why? According to Discovery Channel television researchers, who made a programme about the find in 2005, this is one of Britain's oldest mysteries. A skull of one of the murdered children is on show at the city museum.

the foundations. The walls which famously surround Canterbury today were actually built in the middle ages. Some old Roman bricks can still be seen in the archways but the stone is mostly from the 11th century.

By the end of the 4th century the Romans returned to Italy to save their crumbling empire. The Cantiaci and the rest of Britain were left to fend for themselves. How long the citizens of Canterbury remained in their city is debatable. Although most historians argue that evidence suggests most people fled from their towns in the 4th century, Sheppard Frere suggests the Roman way life in Canterbury went on well into the 5th century. This is despite the raids and incursions on Britain by Germanic tribes of the Dark Ages. Tradition says that the attacks on Kent were led by the legendary brothers Hengist and Horsa, who were Jutes, in 450. The coin discovered in the old Bath House in St George's Street dates back to this time, along with other artefacts including pieces of pottery now on show at the Roman Museum.

At present there is little information about how long Roman Canterbury existed under the attacks, and later the settlement, of Saxon raiders. Various discoveries of valuable Roman artefacts carefully stored underground (like the treasured silver spoon collection) tell us that some residents trying to escape the assaults felt they might come back one day to reclaim their valuables, although apparently they never did so.

A visit to the Museum of Canterbury shows two wonderfully illustrative graphic images of the city as a bustling Roman enterprise full of homes and life. Another picture shows a scene of mass dereliction, with a crumbling Roman theatre and a few pieces of stone to earmark where a much loved home had once been. This image is believed to show how the city looked between the time that the Romans left and the time when the Germanic settlers moved in around a hundred years later.

'Durovernum Cantiacorum' then became the territory of the invaders, commonly referred to as the Anglo-Saxons. These people built their homes out of wood and made roofs out of sturdy thatch. Around this time in the 6th century the area of Kent is believed to have been ruled by a king called Guoyrancgonus. His people worked and constructed their lives around the Roman

THE MUSEUM OF CANTERBURY 2005
C18704k (Simon Hildrew)

The museum was formerly the Poor Priests' Hospital.

ruins. Pottery believed to date back to the time of the earliest Anglo-Saxon period was discovered last century under the Whitefriars area of the city. According to Sheppard Frere, all this indicates that the city of Canterbury was continuously populated, despite the bleak times of the Dark Ages, although the flimsiness of many Saxon buildings meant

AN ARTIST'S IMPRESSION OF SAXON HOUSES F6015

very little remained of them to be seen in later excavations.

In fact many of today's buildings in the city continue to celebrate links with the Roman era. Grand pillars and archways with Roman bricks remain part of the city's architecture. Anyone who visits the ground floor of Waterstone's bookshop in St Margaret's Street can see behind glass the remains of the city's Roman baths. The baths would have played a huge part in the city's social life and all matters of the heart and mind were discussed through warm steam and relaxing waters.

There is a wonderfully wry section of a text by the Roman writer Seneca who reports on the anguish of a resident who lived above some baths. Seneca recounts how the poor chap got hardly any rest, as the shouts of joy coming from the mouths of boisterous Roman bathers were so loud they filled the air day and night.

Today such is the interest in the city's Roman history that there is a full-time archaeological trust, based at 92a Broad Street. Staff are always pleased to give talks to interested parties and give out information about current or future digs in and around the city, and the superb Museum of Canterbury in Stour Street has a host of treasures depicting the city through the ages.

ST MARTIN'S CHURCH 1866 3383

ST MARTIN'S CHURCH, THE FONT 1888 21406

ST MARTIN'S CHURCH, QUEEN BERTHA'S TOMB
1898 40851

In 597 Pope Gregory became concerned about the spiritual well-being of those souls who lived in what he still thought of as the Roman province of Britannia. Gregory called on Augustine, a monk from his own monastery, to travel to 'Durovernum Cantiacorum' (soon to become Cantwaraburh) with a group of fellow Christians to establish the word of God there and build a church. At first Augustine was against the idea because he was afraid of the hostility he would meet from the Saxons when he reached the shores of Kent. But after listening to Pope Gregory's words of encouragement Augustine and his fellow monks set sail and on arrival were welcomed by the King of Kent, Ethelbert, and his wife Queen Bertha. The Frankish born Bertha was already a practising Christian, and her husband had presented her with St Martin's Church (as chronicled by Bede). This church, possibly the oldest in Britain, has a chancel which has Roman features. It was named after St Martin, the patron saint of Tours, the French town in which Bertha had grown up.

St Martin's Church was the place where St Augustine and his monks based themselves soon after arriving in Canterbury in 597. An expansion to St Martin's took place in the 7th century and evidence of this building work is visible by looking at the nave and the windows on the west side.

It was Ethelbert who donated the land where today's majestic cathedral now stands.

For many years St Augustine's Abbey (the site is on the road to Richborough) was the prime place of worship in Canterbury. It contained the bones of saints and archbishops, including the remains of the devout Queen Bertha. Benedictine monks set up the abbey church, dedicated to St Peter and St Paul. In 978 St Dunstan rededicated the abbey to St Augustine.

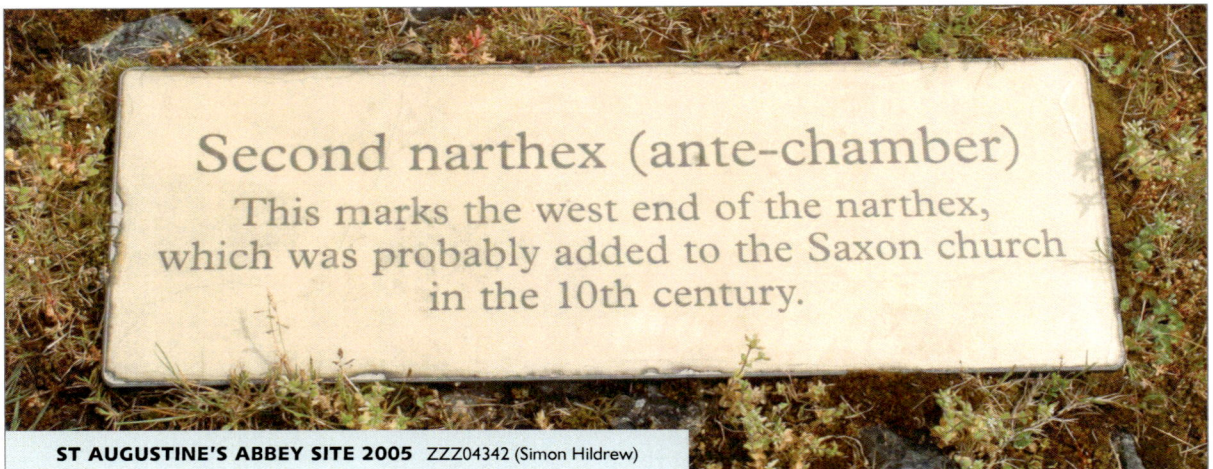

Second narthex (ante-chamber)
This marks the west end of the narthex, which was probably added to the Saxon church in the 10th century.

ST AUGUSTINE'S ABBEY SITE 2005 ZZZ04342 (Simon Hildrew)

ST AUGUSTINE'S ABBEY SITE 2005 ZZZ04341 (Simon Hildrew)

Other smaller churches on the site, like St Gregory's, also held the tombs of archbishops, including the first ones - Augustine, Laurentius, Mellitus, Justus, Honorius and Deusdedit. At St Martin's there were royal tombs and a church dedicated to St Pancras, to the east of the site, contained Roman bricks.

The ruins of this particular church, which can still be seen, give the visitor a good insight into what the monks and their Abbot Wulfric tried to achieve architecturally in 1050. Today this ancient site is made up of mounds of stones, remains of old walls and derelict foundations, but its history as a very early place of worship is preserved and pinpointed as a key visitor site by English Heritage. According to historians, it played a major part in showing us how Christians from ancient Rome liked to have an estate outside the city walls in which to consort and discuss business as well as worship.

Later, many of the shrines at the abbey site were removed and installed at the cathedral when it was rebuilt by the Normans.

Ethelbert's successful trade dealings with the Franks greatly impressed Pope Gregory. The Pope knew this communication between

THE CATHEDRAL, ARCHBISHOP ARCHIBALD TAIT'S MONUMENT 1888 21382a

Archibald Campbell Tait was Archbishop of Canterbury from 1868-1883. This picture was taken in 1888.

the two coastal areas of Europe would be of great advantage to the cause of Christianity, and that ideally an old Roman city would be the best place to establish a significant base from which to begin a huge public relations mission to spread the word of God throughout England (as it was now becoming) and the rest of Europe. Although there had been a Christian presence in the Roman province of Britannia this has been largely submerged by the wave of Germanic immigration, and a new missionary campaign was needed.

Pope Gregory wanted existing Roman buildings or established religious sites (whether Christian or pagan) to form centres for this renewed Christian worship, and Augustine sought out these with gusto, settling initially on the site that was to became St Augustine's Abbey.

But for several decades during the reign of the first few archbishops, Canterbury's importance as a seat of Christianity waned. There was a plague in 664, which killed many clergy and caused people to turn back to their old gods; paganism started to take hold once more over the local people. However, the city remained all-important to the papacy. In 668 Pope Vitalian appointed as Archbishop the 67-year-old Theodore of Tarsus, a Greek monk and scholar. He sought to transform the English church and ensure the city reigned ecclesiastically supreme once again. A passion to spread the word, and to encourage the study not only of theology but also of languages and history, prompted Theodore to build a school in c669, to which came a host of young scholars from all over Europe. In 1086 the Domesday Book would record that, by Theodore's time, 36 manors had been already been set up out of the 89 that existed when the book was compiled.

By around the year 800 Canterbury became the home of several mints making coins for King Offa of Essex, St Augustine's community and the Saxon kingdom of Kent, then ruled by Cuthred. It was this king who pioneered a new penny bearing his portrait. Soon the area began to prosper, with extensions to various parts of the city, including the cathedral precinct, being made.

Artefacts from this period include coins from the 8th century and rare Saxon hair combs. A large amount of pottery also indicated what life was like in the city during these times.

But why did Canterbury become the seat of Christianity in England? The answer is that it was historical accident. Pope Gregory envisaged two archbishoprics in England, one based in London and one in York, which would take turns in being in charge. However Essex, including London, turned pagan after King Ethelbert's death in 606, which prevented London becoming

> # *Did you know?*
> *In 1011 Archbishop Alphege was pelted to death with ox bones by Danish raiders because he refused to surrender and have a ransom paid for him. He was later made a saint and a monument for him can be seen in Canterbury Cathedral.*

an archbishopric. Paganism also returned to York, resulting in the Celtic form of Christianity becoming dominant in that area. Canterbury then became the principal archbishopric- indeed the only one for some time - simply because there was nowhere else suitable.

When the alarming and feisty Danes sailed into the Kent coast and launched attacks on Canterbury between 835 and 1012 many locals died, even though their families continued to defend the city and its places of Christian worship. But times were tense. A few decades later the Danes began blackmailing the city and requested all valuables from the city's places of worship. These were handed over to them. A battle raged, and a great fire broke out, which wiped out all work on the cathedral. St Augustine's Abbey was spared. There is a suggestion that there had been some bartering between Abbot Aelfmar and the Vikings as the abbot remained free, while an enraged Archbishop Alphege was taken away by the Danes to Greenwich and pelted to death with ox bones during drunken revelry, all because he would not allow a ransom to be paid for him. His death meant Canterbury had acquired another saint and St Alphege was enshrined at St Augustine's Abbey. When the Danish Cnut later became King of England, he gave embarrassed orders that a church dedicated to St Mildred be built within the city walls.

When we stop and think at this point we can understand why the current Dean of the cathedral, Robert Willis, says the worshipping community is in fact one of the oldest and most treasured in Britain. 'Treasured' because of the enormous evidence of how the peoples of Canterbury fought to keep their hallowed places of worship - how they battled through the ravages of time to keep their home turf as the place in which Christianity seriously took off in England.

In other parts of Britain a Christian Church had survived during the Dark Ages in Wales, Devon, Cornwall, Cumbria, and in Strathclyde after the Saxon settlement. More missionaries had also come from Ireland, regenerating the Church in the north of England. However, the Roman model (led in England by Canterbury) became predominant after the Synod of Whitby in 663.

THE DEANERY c1868 4173

WESTGATE AND ST DUNSTAN'S STREET c1955 C18047

This street was named after Archbishop Dunstan (960-988)

CATHEDRAL SPOKESMAN, CHRISTOPHER ROBINSON
2005 ZZZ04117 (Melody Ryall)

Today's helpful cathedral spokesman Christopher Robinson says: 'The Dean, Robert Willis, knows the cathedral has been in Canterbury for 900 years but the community has come to this site for more than 1400 years to pray. That makes this community older than the monarchy, and older than any university establishment in Britain. It is a unique and wonderful fact that it is the people who down the ages have kept Christianity alive at Canterbury and at the cathedral.'

Way back in the 6th and 7th centuries, Augustine sent regular letters from Canterbury to the Pope in Rome asking for advice about how to deal with certain spiritual and challenging situations. Cathedral spokesman Mr Robinson says: 'I am sure by the time those missives reached the Pope Augustine would have had time to work out his problems for himself anyway!'

However, despite the great message of faith and hope spun out by Augustine and his followers down the ages nothing would stop the invading Normans from storming Canterbury in the 11th century.

Who knows why these men in their helmets and nose protectors swung on their chain mail, sailed the Channel and set their sights on the lands in England? Generations of men whatever their country of origin always feel the need to seek and conquer new territories, and William of Normandy promised land and power to those who would join him in his Conquest of England. Just as the Romans and the Vikings had done, so the Normans came crashing through the gates of the town the Saxons had christened Canterwara-byrig (or the burh of the Cantwara, the men of Kent).

Today Martin Crowther is Canterbury Museums' assistant senior curator. He reckons that, despite the Normans' determination to storm in and seize territory beyond their homeland, they did ultimately have a positive impact on the city because of their building and masonry skills.

'Great stonework was constructed by them soon after they landed here. Canterbury got a castle, the cathedral was rebuilt and the monasteries were all built of stone. The impact they had on the area is still very much in evidence today, especially at the cathedral. Much of this work, which formed the basis of the whole structure, was instigated by Archbishop Lanfranc.'

It has been well chronicled that in 1067 a huge fire obliterated the cathedral and wiped out its many historic gold and silver objets d'art and rare manuscripts. The Norman builders, financed by William I, set themselves a challenge to recreate a great mother church. Over the years great strides were made on the construction of the cathedral and extensions, and the re-shaping began to create a great impact on the Canterbury skyline. However, all the good work went up in smoke in 1174, when yet another fire wiped out most of the new features.

At the cathedral some small parts of the original Norman rebuild still remain in the crypt and the quire along with a small tower on the south-east transept.

It wasn't only the cathedral that was rebuilt after the blaze of 1067. The second half of the 11th century saw the creation of monasteries in the city. Archbishop Lanfranc was famed for writing a rulebook for monks, including a chapter which mentioned that bath time only came around five times a year! The Normans were also great believers in training children to join the priesthood and many youngsters were given over to the local abbots to train, from the age of just ten years old.

THE CATHEDRAL c1888 21350

These developments would, no doubt, have had the authorisation of a powerful man named Odo. He was the half-brother of King William (the Conqueror) and acted as regent when the king was not in England.

After the Norman Conquest of 1066, King William's half-brother Odo, Bishop of Bayeux, was made Earl of Kent. It was Bishop Odo who commissioned the Bayeux Tapestry (actually an embroidery) to depict the events of the conquest, probably to display at the dedication of his new cathedral in Bayeux in 1077. Stylistic and textual analysis of the Bayeux Tapestry has led many scholars to believe that it was made in Canterbury, where there was a famous school at the time which was renowned all over western Europe for producing large-scale needleworks depicting narratives in pictorial form. The work, which appears to have been made in 'the Canterbury tradition', was probably designed by one person, and created by a group of nuns who were highly skilled in such work.

Some historians claim this as fact because not only is Odo featured on the famous wall hanging, but so is a local man named Vitalis.

Assistant senior curator of the City Museums, Martin Crowther, says Vitalis was a scout who let William and his armies know King Harold and his men were on their way to Hastings to do battle.

Some say that Odo commissioned the tapestry to celebrate his half-brother's win at the Battle of Hastings. According to the

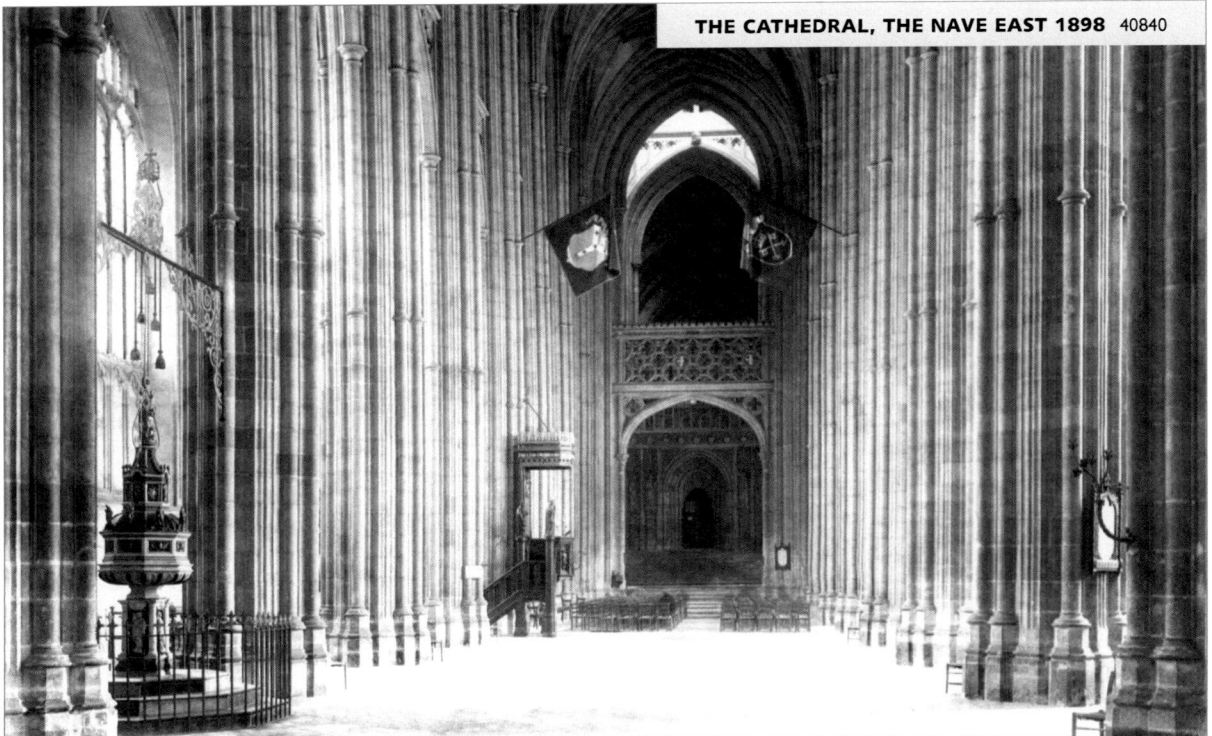

THE CATHEDRAL, THE NAVE EAST 1898 40840

Canterbury Archive the scout, Vitalis, was a local man who owned land in Canterbury and Whitstable. He was also a friend of Wadard who played a key organisational role in the famous Hastings clash.

In 1070 crafty Odo had a terrific row with Canterbury's Archbishop Lanfranc over land ownership, and in the years to come relations between the two became more than frosty. Eventually, after persuading several Norman barons to support him in his greed for lands and property, Odo was jailed for sedition. When William died the scheming Odo tried to lead a revolt but was captured and held at Rochester Castle. Eventually he died in 1097, on his way to a crusade.

Did you know?

Archbishop Lanfranc believed a flint struck from a minter working near the cathedral sparked, catching alight dry material nearby, and setting fire to the cathedral. So the said minter was then moved away from the cathedral precinct to work, and was offered a home at what was then the Poor Priests' Hospital. This building now houses the Museum of Canterbury.

THE CATHEDRAL TODAY 2005   C18705k (Simon Hildrew)

THE CATHEDRAL, THE CHOIR EAST 1890 25688a

In 1170 Archbishop Thomas Becket was murdered in the cathedral after a long-running argument with King Henry II. Three years after Thomas's death he was canonized. Money flowed into the cathedral's coffers, from gifts and from the pilgrims who visited the tomb of the saint. Two architects, William of Sens and (after the former's death in an accident) William the Englishman, oversaw a reconstruction of the cathedral on a massive scale that included the building of two wonderful new towers. This magnificent place of worship, that still holds the title of mother church of the Anglican Communion, soon became the jewel in the city's crown.

The reasons are manifold. It truly is a shrine and a celebration of Christianity and its amazing architecture seduces the eye with its varied styles and forms.

Cathedral spokesman Christopher Robinson says: 'The building itself is a bit of a hotch-potch, actually. There are parts constructed during the time of several archbishops: Lanfranc in 1070, then St Anselm in 1096 and Wibert in 1153. Anselm and Wibert oversaw the creation of the Chapter House, north-east transept, part of the quires and the south-east transept.'

In 1993 Canterbury Archaeological Trust carried out a dig in the first nave when re-flooring was carried out to accommodate

THE CATHEDRAL, THE TRANSEPT OF MARTYRDOM 1890 25689

THE CATHEDRAL, THE BELL HARRY TOWER 1888
21359

CHRIST CHURCH GATE c1955 C18052

The bronze statue of Christ had yet to be installed when this photograph was taken.

new heating facilities. They discovered much evidence of a Saxon cathedral, and foundations indicating alterations to the crypt. The Saxons had reused Roman stone in parts and some of this was also used by the Normans in the early part of the 11th century.

Small additions to this work were commissioned by Archbishop Richard in 1175, the architect being William of Sens, then Trinity Chapel and the Corona Chapel were constructed under the orders of William the Englishman in 1179. The 13th century saw the creation of a library and the noble quire was added, with a key amount of building work being carried out in the north and south aisle of the nave in the 15th century. Much money was spent on the cathedral by the Kings of England, including Henry VII who reigned when the distinctive and noble Bell Harry Tower was built in 1498.

TOMBS IN THE WARRIORS' CHAPEL c1862 1087

This is always a popular meeting place for city residents and tourists alike. The magnificent Christ Church Gate that majestically greets most visitors is resplendent in Gothic glory. It was built in 1517 by Prior Thomas Goldstone, whose coat of arms is visible at the front. Restoration work took place on Christ Church Gate between 1931 and 1937, after the city surveyor expressed concern about the strength and safety of the turrets. It was thanks to two cathedral benefactors, the sisters Dame Janet Stancomb-Wills and Yda Richardson, and their donation of more than £7,000, that the tallest parts of this magnificent and historic gate were replaced. These 'new' Gothic-style turrets were unveiled by Dr George Bell, the former dean of the cathedral (and also the man who devised the first ever Canterbury Festival in 1929).

CHRIST CHURCH GATE IN 2005 C18706k (Simon Hildrew)

In the 19th and 20th century the north aisle of the nave was reconstructed to help accommodate one of the 53 monuments, that of Archbishop Benson, who led the church from 1883 to 1897.

Today's Archbishop, Dr Rowan Williams, is the 104th to hold the position. He is, according to spokesman Mr Robinson, a man who enjoys visiting small parishes just as much as preaching a sermon at the cathedral.

Mr Robinson explains: 'The marvellous thing about the cathedral is how it embraces everyone. The pilgrims were a mixture of all sorts of people from all sorts of different backgrounds as Chaucer so brilliantly pointed out in his 'Canterbury Tales'. The stained glass is a real wonder for visitors, and is believed to be the finest 12th-century stained glass in Europe, along with the high quality Gothic architecture.'

THE CATHEDRAL, THE CHOIR EAST 1890 25688a

In fact some of the most remarkable coloured glass can be seen in the Trinity Chapel, where a magnificent and much visited shrine to Thomas Becket once stood. There are four panels on the fourth window on the north aisle. One depicts a sleeping King of France as he dreamed of Becket - the martyr he once shielded from the soldiers of Henry II.

Much is done to educate young visitors. Theatre has played an important role in presenting the history of the cathedral and all it stands for. T S Eliot wrote a famous play, 'Murder in the Cathedral', that focuses on the story of the murder of Archbishop Thomas Becket in 1170. This play never fails to attract young and old whenever it is performed. And although, according to Dr Kenneth Pickering, local academic and author of the book 'Drama in the Cathedral', plays were sometimes seen as a con to get people into church, there is a close unity between religious drama and the teachings of Christianity.

Dr Pickering, who lives in Canterbury and is a noted director of medieval plays, writes: 'By the second half of the nineteenth century, the antagonism between the Church and Stage seemed irreconcilable. Yet, within a few decades, Canterbury Cathedral was enticing such literary giants as Masefield, Binyon, Eliot and Sayers to write plays for performance in the Cathedral precincts.'

There are three full-time educational officers at the cathedral. With a huge number of visitors seeking out the cathedral (1,091,000 visitors in 2004) these members of staff play a vital role in the health and future of the precinct. Most of the visitors to the cathedral are European.

Until 1540 there were monks in residence in the cathedral precincts, but when Henry VIII closed all the monasteries most had to take a pension or become part of the new administrative regime.

However, 300 years earlier the arrival of a few Franciscan friars caused some interest and laid the foundations of the presence of their order in England. Nine Franciscans got off a ship at Dover in 1224 and when they

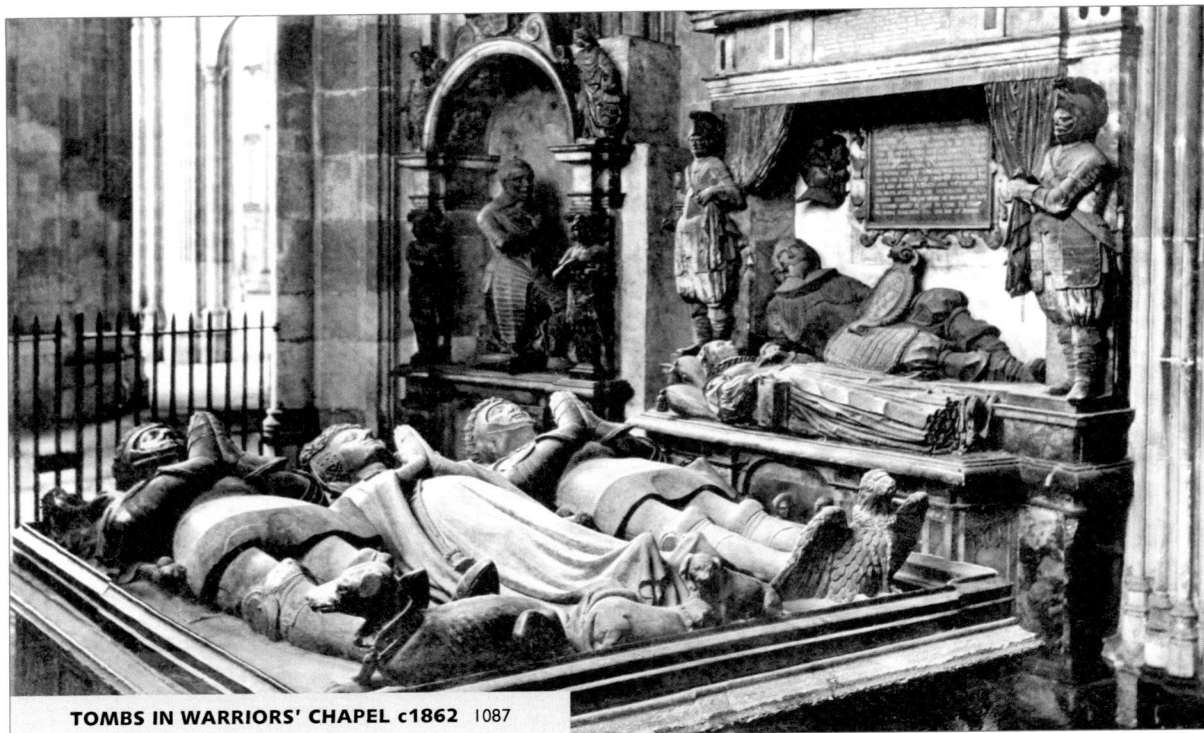

TOMBS IN WARRIORS' CHAPEL c1862 1087

reached Canterbury five of them stayed at the Poor Priests' Hospital in Stour Street.

From Canterbury, the Franciscans later moved on to London and then to Oxford, building up their numbers all the time. In 1973 they returned to Canterbury and today they are based at the Franciscan International Study Centre close to the University of Kent.

In 1221 the city saw the arrival of the Dominican friars who became known as 'Blackfriars' because over the top of their white habits they sported a black coat. A friary for them was created on an island in the River Stour given to them by Henry III in 1237. It was one of two buildings. Today, tourists who take the popular trip up river can still see the magnificent building that the

Blackfriars once occupied.

Other groups of friars that set up home in Canterbury over the centuries included the Greyfriars and Whitefriars.

When the shrine of Thomas Becket was destroyed in 1538 Archbishop Whitgift had an Act of Parliament passed which ordered that that the Eastbridge Hospital (originally built in the 13th century to house pilgrims who visited Becket's shrine) should accommodate ten poor people of the city. In 2005 almshouses linked to the old hospital are occupied by elderly residents with strong links to Canterbury. The old Eastbridge Hospital is open to visitors on most days.

Such open doors also exist at the world famous cathedral each day.

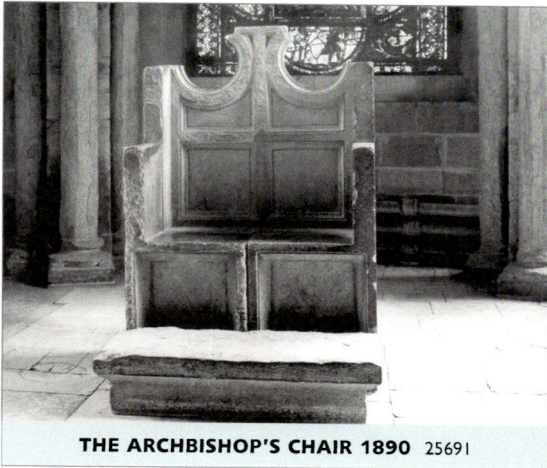

THE ARCHBISHOP'S CHAIR 1890 25691

Today's cathedral staff embrace the media as much as they can - unlike their predecessors of 1944, who were not at all happy about allowing film director Michael Powell to set some of his classic film 'The Canterbury Tale' in the nave.

However anyone who has seen this film will know that Powell won the argument. We are offered a wonderful scene in which one of the soldier characters, who is an organ scholar in peacetime, is allowed to play Bach's Toccata in D Minor to all the troops awaiting service. It is a moving moment as the great chords ring out, and Powell was right to fight for the chance to set this scene in such majestic surroundings.

The last big event at the cathedral was the enthronement of the Archbishop, Dr Rowan Williams, in 2003. For this occasion the BBC set monitors all over the cathedral to ensure not one moment was missed. Each enthronement has involved the BBC. Before the arrival of television cameras these historic occasions could be heard live on the radio.

THE TOMB OF HENRY IV 1888 21380

Why do people still flock to Canterbury Cathedral? Cathedral spokesman Mr Robinson says it is the anonymity of the place. This author agrees. There is something so hallowed, so serene, so historic and so lauded about this extraordinary building that many of the woes of the 21st-century visitor take second place to the sufferings in the lives of those that are either buried there or remembered by plaques, memorials and prayers.

CHAPTER TWO

The Making of a Martyr

FOR ANYONE interested in the world of public relations, the cathedral has an inbuilt superstar who never fails to attract the visitors in their millions. This extraordinary man has already been described by some as the Marlon Brando of the place. His life and death in the 12th century were just about as dramatic as anything any Hollywood superstar could have starred in!

> The story of Thomas Becket, Archbishop of Canterbury, was the subject of a big screen epic in 1964, starring Richard Burton as the 'meddlesome' priest and Peter O'Toole as his adversary and former friend, Henry II. This film, 'Becket', was an adaptation of Jean Anouilh's play of the same name: and at the time of its release and just like its subject, it made an impact on audiences all over the world, winning a host of glittering awards.

The real Thomas Becket, however, was born in London on 21 December 1118. Unlike the character in the film version he was not a Saxon, but of Norman-French parentage. He studied at the University of Paris.

His first encounter with Canterbury came in 1141, when he was given a clerk's position by Theobald, Archbishop of Canterbury. A description of the young Becket was recorded and he is described as slim and pale with a long nose and dark hair. The 12th-century chronicler of the appearance of the saint-to-be also mentions a man who made lovable

conversation, was frank speaking with a slight stutter, and who had an extraordinary ability to turn difficult questions and situations into a new dimension of wisdom.

The story goes that Theobald was soon full of admiration for his young clerk and despatched him abroad to study civil and canon law. In 1154 Becket achieved deacon status. Within months, the newly crowned 24-year-old King Henry II had met and become firm friends with the 36-year-old Becket.

Henry II made his friend Thomas Becket chancellor, and together they strove to build a united England. They even fought battles together. Some historians say the young Becket was a mean warrior when he wanted to be and had no qualms about attacking and slaying enemies on the battlefield. Henry and Becket shared their pleasures: hunting, women, feasting and much jovial conversation. Their bonding was evident for the whole of England to see - until 1161.

> In the 12th century Britain's oldest working bridge was created - the King's Bridge, which sits over the River Stour in the High Street, and until 1970 supported all the heavy traffic on its way through Canterbury to reach Dover. To see beneath this amazing bridge, which sits next to the medieval Weavers' House, the author recommends one of Carey's boat trips. These go around the city to the Franciscan island. (More about this essential tourist trip can be found in a later chapter.)

A VIEW OF THE WEAVERS' HOUSE c1955 C18063

ALONG THE RIVER STOUR 2005
C18707k (Simon Hildrew)

This is the view from just past the old Weavers' House.

THE OLD WEAVERS' HOUSE 2005
C18708k (Simon Hildrew)

The Weavers' House is in the High Street - today it is a busy restaurant.

In 1161 the then Archbishop and Becket's old mentor, Theobald, died. Henry who believed he was doing the right thing for the country, decided Becket must be made a priest and take over the Archbishop's post. Henry thought that if he put his own man at the helm of the mother church, then the wearing struggles over land, taxes and power between the King and the church which had been plaguing him would be over! How wrong he was.

Henry II was so desperate to see Becket as Archbishop he even paid the monks of Canterbury to vote his old friend into the top job. But at first Becket, who still wore his chancellor's hat, turned down the offer to be Archbishop. Henry declared Becket's opposition as 'nonsense' and continued to insist his friend take on the role. Becket eventually agreed to become Archbishop, and he was consecrated on 3 June 1162. At the time he said to his royal friend prophetically: 'I know your plans for the Church, you will

GREY FRIARS 1924 76111

assert claims which I, if I were Archbishop, must oppose!'

There are also the meaningful words he said to a friend on the way to his ordination: 'Hereafter, I want you to tell me, candidly and in secret, what people are saying about me. And if you see anything in me that you regard as a fault, feel free to tell me in private. For from now on, people will talk about me, but not to me. It is dangerous for men in power if no one dares to tell them when they go wrong.'

But from the day Becket wore the holy mitre and began his reign at the cathedral, hostilities began between him and Henry. At first it was put down to misunderstandings, but as soon as Becket realised that Henry's plan was to bring the might of the Church under the rule of the King, tempers flared. Becket hit back and opposed his old friend the King.

In 1164 Henry declared he wanted the right to try criminous clerks. He said those accused of felony should face their charge in a lay court, then be given over to a church court. If at this trial they were found guilty then they would be stripped of holy orders and taken back to the King's lay court for punishment and sentencing.

Henry's desire to add this procedure to the constitution is reasonable enough. He felt this would ensure that no-one could escape the might of the law, not even if they were part of the church. As it stood at that time, anyone with holy orders who committed a crime often escaped punishment.

A meeting of barons and clergy was held at the palace of Clarendon, south of Salisbury in Wiltshire. This meeting resulted in a document that defined the powers of Church and State, which became known as the Constitutions of Clarendon. Henry wanted Becket to sign this agreement. When Becket picked up the pen he hesitated for a few seconds then threw it down in anger. He refused to add his name to it.

Becket left the meeting and, pursued by the wrath of the King, he left England and escaped to Rouen in France. He was welcomed by King Louis VII and promptly informed Pope

Alexander in Rome of Henry's wishes. But an intransigent Becket refused to give up one iota of the Church's authority.

During his years as Archbishop there is little doubt Becket thoroughly got into his role as shepherd of the flock. He was devoted to the Church, Christianity and all it represented. He rid himself of riches and wealth and gave most of his belongings to the poor; he told the King he no longer wished to be Chancellor; he took to wearing hair shirts and he embraced a life of humility and repentance. He often starved himself and deprived his body of sleep in an effort to get closer to God. There is also a record of him walking the streets of Canterbury at night to help the lepers, beggars and the sick. It is thanks to Becket that hospices for pilgrims and travellers were built in the city.

In 1170 when Becket was still exiled in France, Pope Alexander threatened to excommunicate Henry, who then panicked; if he was to be excommunicated no-one would be obliged to obey him, resulting in a serious threat to his authority. It was suggested there must be a diplomatic answer to the conflicts between Henry and his Archbishop and an amicable solution could be worked out between them. However, this was not a real way forward to solving such mighty differences of opinion, and on Becket's return to Canterbury on 3 December 1170, hostilities between the two men flared up again.

Becket's followers were anxious. The situation was tense. Edward Grim, a Becket admirer, is quoted in medieval source books as a witness of what happened next.

The story that follows led to Becket's martyrdom and confirmed his 'medieval superstar' status. According to chroniclers of the time Henry hosted a dinner at which he was overheard to say of Becket: 'Who will rid me of this meddlesome priest!'

THE PILGRIMS' HOSPITAL 2005   C18709k (Simon Hildrew)

The Pilgrims' Hospital of St Thomas is in the High Street, opposite the ancient King's Bridge.

The tone of the question has been the subject of much controversy down the ages. Did the king say it as an expression of frustration to his assembled dinner guests or did he aim and intend it to be heard by his faithful swordsmen in the full knowledge they would act out his wish and assassinate Becket?

But at the time four knights loyal to their King (Reginald FitzUrze, Hugh de Morville, William de Tracey and Richard le Breton) took it upon themselves to assassinate Becket. On 29 December 1170, with the help of various malicious monks, they called out for him at the cathedral. They cried: 'Where is Thomas Becket, traitor of the King and kingdom?'

Becket was preparing to celebrate vespers when he heard them. He is believed to have replied: 'The righteous will be like a bold lion and free from fear. Here I am, not a traitor to the King but a priest: why do you seek me?'

The knights then demanded Becket absolve those he had excommunicated but Becket refused, and after a struggle he bent down to pray with his head bowed. One of his assassins, the knight Richard FitzUrze, became so enraged he sliced his sword through the air to land on the Archbishop's head. After three blows to Becket's head the top of his skull was cut off, causing his brains to spill out. A fifth assassin, described as an 'evil cleric' by Edward Grim, who was wounded trying to prevent Becket's murder, then stamped on the Archbishop's neck so the brains spewed out in all directions.

Did you know?

It has been suggested that Becket was not exactly an easy man to know. He could be difficult, arrogant and bossy. He used his knowledge of the law to act in a superior way at times and was often aloof with those he believed of inferior intellect. He has even been called a 'curmudgeon' and rather dour by historians.

Grim records how the Archbishop was slain like a sacrificial lamb, but that during his bloody murder never once did he cry out. The last words he was believed to have said were: 'I accept death for the name of Jesus and for the Church.'

But the story doesn't end there. Three years after Becket died at the age of 52, the Pope canonised him. King Henry's guilt over his old friend's death seized him with such force that in 1174 he felt compelled to ask for forgiveness. The King then did penance at Becket's shrine in the cathedral and was flogged by monks. Becket's bones were transported to Trinity Chapel in 1220 until they were plundered and destroyed during Henry VIII's Dissolution of the Monasteries in the 16th century.

The number of pilgrims who sought out Becket's shrine between the reigns of Henry II and Henry VIII was phenomenal. Indeed, the cathedral steps that lead to the place in Trinity Chapel where the martyr's bones lay are worn from centuries of the footsteps of the faithful, and of their kneeling in prayer.

THE CATHEDRAL, TRINITY CHAPEL 1888 21377

In 1500 the shrine was visited by Polydore Vergil, a Venetian. He described what he saw: 'The tomb of St Thomas the martyr, Archbishop of Canterbury, exceeds all belief. Notwithstanding its great size, it is wholly covered with plates of pure gold; yet the gold is scarcely seen because it is covered by various precious stones, as sapphires, balasses, diamonds, rubies, and emeralds; and whenever the eye turns something more beautiful than the rest is observed.

Nor in additional to these natural beauties, is the skill of art wanting, for in the midst of the gold are the most beautiful sculptured gems both small and large, as well such as are in relief as, agates, onyxes, cornelians, cameos; and some cameos are of such size that I am afraid to name it; but everything is far surpassed by a ruby, not larger than a thumbnail, which is fixed at the right of the altar.

The church is somewhat dark, and particularly the spot where the shrine is placed, and when we went to see it the sun was near setting, and the weather was cloudy; nevertheless I saw that ruby as if I had it in my hand. They say it was given by a King of France.'

This 'great ruby' was more likely a diamond (otherwise called the 'Regale of France') given to the shrine by King Louis VII when he made a pilgrimage to Canterbury in 1179. It was Louis who had helped protect Becket when he was in exile in France. This magnificent jewel however somehow ended up encased in a gold ring, which later Henry VIII wore on his thumb.

The base of the shrine is described as being of pink marble, and pilgrims were able to touch the coffin containing Becket's remains.

The great scholar and thinker Erasmus claims he saw the actual items removed from Becket's body, which had been left at the first tomb in the crypt. Erasmus said he was shown the hair shirt (which had been infested with lice), Becket's skull and some drawers.

The spot where Becket fell and the place his head hit the ground is marked by a white tile with black edges. A dramatic sculpture of a jagged cross supporting two swords, one with a broken tip, sits on the wall reminding visitors they are on special and famous ground.

For many years part of Becket's skull lay in a monument in the Corona Chapel (so named after the crown of the head) in the cathedral. The Corona Chapel was constructed in 1179 under the auspices of Archbishop Richard in the north west transept as a dedication to 'modern' martyrs.

Henry VIII came to the throne 369 years after Becket's death and this led to the desecration of the famous shrine because of the King's hostility over the martyr's 'audacity' to champion the cause of Christianity over royal rule. The Act for the dissolution of the greater monasteries was in 1539, occasioned mainly because Henry VIII came into conflict with the Church over his desire for a divorce that the Pope denied him.

An academic, Thomas Cranmer, who supported the king was appointed Archbishop of Canterbury in 1533, and Parliament passed an Act that said all appeals of spiritual matters should go to Cranmer in Canterbury and not to Rome. An outraged Pope then excommunicated Henry and Cranmer and the King passed a law in 1533/4 making the Church of England independent of Rome. This put the monks of England in a terrible position. How could they be loyal to a Pope and a King? The crafty monarch though wanted their money and allowed the desecration of Becket's tomb and other religious shrines all over the land that were laden with jewels and gold.

An exact date to mark the destruction of Becket's tomb is difficult to pinpoint. Some historians reckon it happened during the year 1538, but it was two years later than Henry's first minister Thomas Cromwell was ordered to take the wealth from Canterbury Cathedral. All ornaments, jewellery and plates were then surrendered to the King.

Henry VIII, who was by then on to his third wife, Jane Seymour, also instituted legal proceedings against the long dead Becket. Henry condemned and ridiculed the saint publicly. There were, said Henry, to be no more festivals in honour of the martyr.

There is a white marble tile marking the spot at the place in the cathedral where Becket died. His head had struck the floor after the crown had been sliced clean off. As life ebbed away from him, that cold winter's day in 1170, Becket lay in a position of prayer until his body was removed. It was later placed in a tomb, which over the next few decades became the most visited and hallowed shrine in medieval England. When the shocked and grieving monks undressed his body to wash it, they discovered that their Archbishop wore a hair shirt, indicating that he wished to share the constant suffering of the poor and lowly.

THE CATHEDRAL, THE SPOT WHERE BECKET DIED, PHOTOGRAPHED IN 2005 C18710k
(Simon Hildrew)

This hallowed white marble tile marks the spot of Becket's death.

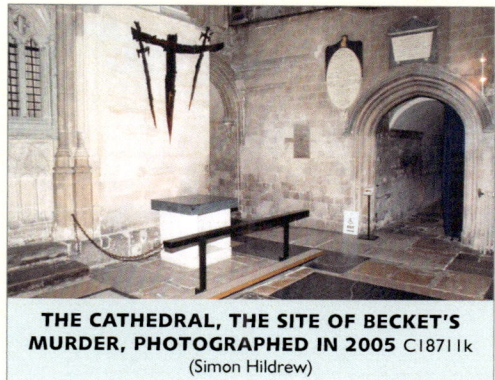

THE CATHEDRAL, THE SITE OF BECKET'S MURDER, PHOTOGRAPHED IN 2005 C18711k
(Simon Hildrew)

Becket's shrine today, at the site of his murder, the most visited part of the mighty cathedral.

Some historians say the King had Becket's bones burned in a bid to stop any further veneration of him.

Others claim the saint's remains were actually hurriedly buried near the cathedral. Mystery still surrounds the day in 1888 when a coffin was discovered in the crypt. Inside the skeleton was that of a tallish man with an injured skull - like the fatal wound inflicted on Becket in 1170. The proof that this is the skeleton of the cathedral's most famous Archbishop has yet to be found. The wonders of today's DNA testing were not available in 1888 - and without the clothes of the murdered martyr, scientists would still not be able to reveal the true identity of the bones in the coffin.

Cathedral spokesman Mr Robinson says: 'The story of Thomas Becket is a huge draw. He was the Marlon Brando of the cathedral history! The star attraction! People are terribly interested in him and his martyrdom. Always have been and always will be. Becket was 52 when he died. This tells us a lot about the man anyway before he was brutally murdered. To reach 52 meant the individual had a very good constitution at a time when there was a great deal of infant mortality. They were terribly

hard times. To survive all the diseases around then a person had to made of strong stuff.'

When this author spoke to visitors at the cathedral she was told Becket was always going to be the main draw for them.

One visitor, Miss Margaret Cutler, who lives in the weald of Kent about 30 miles to the north of Canterbury, said: 'My visit to Becket's tomb is prompted by his link with Eynsford, a village close to my home. In the 11th century William Fitzralph, lord of the 'soil' of Eynsford, handed over the church of St Martin at Eynsford to Christ Church, Canterbury. When Becket appointed a priest to St Martin's, William de Eynesford turned him out and an enraged Becket excommunicated the lord of Eynsford Castle. The knight then appealed to his friend the King and the Archbishop gave way, but it was the beginning of the end for Becket.

Shortly after he was killed at the cathedral. Whilst de Eynesford was not one of the four knights who murdered Becket, following the Archbishop's death William de Eynesford was filled with remorse and gave us his castle to join the monks.'

In 1982, Pope John Paul II became the first-ever pontiff to visit Canterbury Cathedral. He arrived by helicopter and more than 25,000 lined the streets to welcome him and wave flags in his honour. The Pope told reporters his visit was 'a day which centuries and generations have awaited'.

On his arrival Archbishop Robert Runcie walked with the Pope to the deanery where they met Prince Charles and leading church figures. They lit candles for many saints, and the Pope and Dr Runcie knelt together in prayer at the spot of Becket's.

At the place where Becket's shrine had once been a candle is lit every day. It seems the might of Becket had even attracted and touched the spiritual might of His Holiness the Pope too.

THE CATHEDRAL, THE PLAQUE AT THE SITE OF THE MURDER OF THOMAS BECKET, PHOTOGRAPHED IN 2005 C18712k (Simon Hildrew)

This plaque, placed near Becket's shrine, records a historic day.

A SECTION OF A MAP OF KENT SHOWING CANTERBURY AND SURROUNDING AREAS c1850

CHAPTER THREE

Cultural Giants

NOW WE MUST return briefly to the 20th century film, 'The Canterbury Tale', mentioned in the introduction to this book. This author has seen no better way of introducing the seductive power and influence Canterbury exerted over our forefathers who decide to journey to its centre.

The film opens with a group of laughing medieval pilgrims making their way on horseback from Southwark to Canterbury. Their light-hearted banter ripples through the air, a lute is playing and their surrounds are the forests and fields. Now, of course, most of this land has now been ploughed up to make way for the humming traffic which speeds up and down the A2 between Greenwich, Dartford, Cobham, Rochester and finally to the city where one of the world's most famous cathedral rests.

The film captures the imagination of the audience quickly and effortlessly, and the times of the storyteller Geoffrey Chaucer begin to take hold of our senses. A falcon is filmed swooping and soaring high into the clouds and then director Michael Powell masterfully captures the sight and sound of a droning Spitfire aeroplane to transport his audience from the medieval pilgrims to the military pilgrims of the Second World War.

If we put the film on pause here we must appreciate why the director made this important cut. It is not only an important time switch, it heralds the very essence of the pilgrims who over the centuries made their way to Canterbury.

Chaucer based his famous 'Canterbury Tales' on the types of characters who rode along the North Downs Way with a song in their heart and one of two missions in mind, to either receive a penance or blessings.

ST PETER'S STREET c1955 C18041

It has been noted by Chaucer scholars that by the time the great medieval writer penned his glorious stories the popularity of Thomas Becket's shrine was waning and the amount of money the Church was receiving from various visiting pilgrim groups was falling fast.

If this is so then Chaucer not only helped revive interest in Becket and Canterbury, he created a special kind of narrative history that has remained hugely influential in the canon of English Literature. His tales have great humour and great humility and they never fail to entertain all those who see them performed on stage or on radio, or read them in print. Here is a telling excerpt:

'Bifel that, in that seson on a day,
In Southwerk at the Tabard as I lay
Redy to wenden on my pilgrimage
To Cuanterbury with ful devout corage,
At night was come into that hostelrye
Wel nyne and twenty in a companye,
Of sundry folk, by aventure y-falle
In felawshipe, and pilgrims were they alle,
That toward Caunterbury wolden ryde.'

Why the Pilgrims' Way, for Chaucer, began in Southwark (the district now also gives its name to a London borough) is interesting. Apparently back in medieval days the only way those travelling from London could cross the river was to go over London Bridge and make a turn right into Southwark. The Tabard Inn (in what is now Borough High Street) was the point in London from which pilgrims started their journey to Canterbury.

This route had been taken many times by pilgrims on their way to Becket's shrine and so Chaucer decided it was as good a place as any from which to set his tale of everyday folk journeying on pilgrimage to Canterbury.

It is believed Chaucer wrote his collection of diverse and unusual stories around 1387. Among the most ribald and earthy is 'The Miller's Tale', a story about a dishonest clerk who tries it on with the carpenter's wife and gets punished in the bawdiest fashion. This particular tale has audiences laughing long and loud, as it concludes with the baring of naked bottom from a top window. 'The Reeve's Tale' is also saucy - perhaps a forerunner to the classic 'Carry On' films of the 20th century! 'The Nun's Priest's Tale' is a fable about a hen, fox and a cock; 'The Pardoner's Tale' is a message warning about the dangers of greed and selfishness. However, the most effervescent of these storytellers has to be the Wife of Bath who tells all her listeners, quite forthrightly and boisterously, all about her five husbands, before launching into her tale about Sir Gawaine and the Loathly Lady.

> # Did you know?
> *One of the best translations of Chaucer's 'Canterbury Tales' was made by Professor Nevill Coghill. It was published in 1951. A superb recording was made by the Music For Pleasure label and distributed by EMI in 1982. Actors Martin Starkie and Prunella Scales play many of the characters.*

To really enjoy the whole Chaucer spectacular this author thoroughly recommends a visit to The Canterbury Tales Experience in St Margaret's Street, set under the roof of the former Norman St Margaret's Church. Entering through wooden doors, visitors are on a medieval walk through the famous tales via a series of tableaux representing the characters. The journey begins at the Tabard Inn in London and there the visitors meet Geoffrey Chaucer and his jolly pilgrims.

Smell the hurly-burly of medieval life and then chance upon the sequence of tales at the centre, which begins with 'The Knight's Tale'. Hear how two young men fall in love with the same pretty girl, but will there be a happy ending?

Next on the journey visitors may giggle aloud at the bawdy story as told by the Miller. When travellers have walked past this episode they reach a grassy orchard where the rosy-cheeked and boisterous Wife of Bath reveals all about her five husbands and answers the eternal question (also posed by Freud): 'What do women really want?' (Today the Wife of Bath would have made a great character for hit television shows like 'Sex and the City'.)

In the cavernous room next door modern-day visitors to this busy city attraction can hear 'The Nun's Priest's Tale' about a farmyard cockerel, a crafty fox, and a hen.

To end the journey we hear 'The Pardoner's Tale' about trickery and death, before finishing our tour at a re-creation of Becket's Tomb - the destination of all the pilgrims.

The Canterbury Tales Experience, owned by Heritage – part of the Continuum Group, is open most of the year and can be found opposite the HMV store in St Margaret's Street.

In all Chaucer wrote nearly 30 tales that are based on the inter-action between humans, including their flaws, weaknesses and peculiar habits. Much of what he wrote back in the 14th century can be applied to the behaviour exhibited by the inhabitants of the 21st century world. Chaucer makes us ask: 'Do people every really change?'

By the time Chaucer was making literary history, the city of Canterbury had a population of around 11,000. The rich and poor were divided up. The wealthy dwelt in the precincts and the financially challenged usually put down roots just outside Northgate and the south of the city.

In the 13th century the monks lived and worked hard, especially once the cult of belief in St Thomas had been invigorated. Stories of how drops of the saint's blood had restored the sick to health went around the world and his martyrdom was revered almost like the second coming.

The city saw much altruism around this time, mostly thanks to the presence of the Franciscan and Dominican friars who encouraged a certain spiritual health in the city that led to prosperity, growth and good relations with London and other key trading towns.

In the 13th century land was given back to the city by the government to provide shelters for the poor which led to the construction of the Eastbridge Hospital, built over the River Stour by Edward Fitzodbold. Next door was the Hospital of St Nicholas and St Katherine, and eventually the two buildings merged to become a resting place for poverty-stricken pilgrims and homeless women seeking shelter and sustenance. Today it is possible to visit this building, now the Museum of Canterbury, and marvel at the ancient beams, hearths, arches and stone walls. There is also a great range of exhibits charting the city's history, and an impressive interactive tour for visitors.

Around 1348 the city was blighted by the destructive and deathly throes of a bubonic plague, the 'Black Death'. Other diseases such as dysentery, typhoid and tuberculosis were endemic, but despite all the illness and death rampaging the streets, development work continued. For a start the nave was constructed at the cathedral and the community began creating a solid support network for the many churches they hallowed inside the city walls. These included St Mildred's, St Peter's, St Dunstan's and St Margaret's. Attention was paid, too, to ways in which the city could keep out invaders. The walls we see today began to take shape.

Westgate is a place visitors can pass through

THE RIVER STOUR AND SITE OF THE OLD DOMINICAN PRIORY 2005   C18713k (Simon Hildrew)

The site of the old Dominican Priory is on the left. It existed from 1315 to 1538.

on their way to visit the tomb of Edward, the Black Prince, the son of Edward III, which is in the cathedral. The prince, who now lies in state in the cathedral, was hugely influential during the famous Hundred Years War between England and France, which thwarted many lives throughout the 14th and 15th centuries.

WESTGATE AND ST DUNSTAN'S STREET 1921 70330

The rag-stone Westgate towers, built around 1380, were given small outlets from which bowmen could fire arrows at advancing enemies. The places where the walls were once connected to the towers can still be seen today. Road designs centuries later disconnected these noble turrets from the rest of the defences. When a curfew bell rang out from the towers at 9pm it meant no one could leave or enter the city, a common medieval practice. In the 18th century the towers served as a jail. Today the structure is a museum boasting weaponry of the First and Second World Wars.

It is still possible to see what are described as 'murder holes' where the city's protectors stood in wait to tip boiling fat on to the heads of any invaders. The greeting for the world's pilgrims is very different today, of course! The only shower awaiting the visitor of the new millennium is the proverbial British rain, which usually lets up in the spring and summer. This author always finds that whether it is raining, snowy, or sunny there is often a chilly - almost ghostly - blast of air sweeping down the High Street and right on through the narrow path by the Westgate. It is here on occasion that the homeless sit huddled in sleeping bags, asking for the price of a cup of tea. I wonder if they would return to beg at the same place if they knew how medieval guards at Westgate organised the hanging of condemned prisoners at the same spot!

Edward, born in 1330, was a great warrior with established links with Canterbury. It is believed he was educated in the city by a Prior Hathbrand. He was given the name 'the Black Prince' not only because he was regarded by the French enemy as a fearless and brave warrior, but also because of the colour of his armour, which may have been painted black to stop it rusting. (Edward's nickname is first recorded in the 16th century.)

In 1362 the soldier Prince Edward married Joan of Kent and their son later became King Richard II, who ruled between 1377 and 1399. Edward, the Black Prince, famous for his victories at the Battles of Crecy and Poitiers, never got to be King as he died a year before his father. But like an image from a Shakespearean play, Edward, the Black Prince was described thus by a fan: 'He showed his valour to the French, piercing horses, laying low the riders, shattering helmets and breaking spears, skilfully parrying blows aimed against him, helping to their feet friends who had fallen, and showing to all an example in well doing.'

Edward's aggression, though, was not always appealing. One act of barbarism worth noting here is how he ordered the slaughter of 3000 civilians at Limoges in 1370. He had the reputation of being a cruel man, and although he impressed his father the King with his battle prowess, his personality could not cope with those who disagreed with him.

Edward's last drawn-out fight in Spain broke his health. His glorious military career ended in despair as he was forced to retreat and bring his tired and sick men back to Bordeaux.

As ruler of Aquitaine Edward also had a fight on his hands with the French who won back their lands. The Black Prince returned to England, ailing and frail, in 1371 and in 1376 he died aged just 46. The Black Prince

THE CATHEDRAL, THE TOMB OF THE BLACK PRINCE 1888 21379

was buried in Canterbury in the autumn of the year he died. The three plumed feathers seen at his tomb are now used as the emblem of the Prince of Wales. Edward's son Richard was crowned King in 1377.

60 years later in 1437 all those who came to pay homage to the Black Prince and Becket found a more compassionate atmosphere in Canterbury. Beggars and lepers would have found bed and board at one of the newly constructed taverns in the city. The Sun Hotel near the Christ Church gate was one of these. Built in the 14th century, it was also the birthplace of the poet John Lyly (1564-1606) and carries a sign which says: 'Sun Hotel formerly known as The Little Inn made famous by Charles Dickens in his travels through Kent'. Three generations of the Cousins family owned the building and in recent years the second floor has been restored to the herringbone brickwork placed there in the 17th century.

Such inns were built to cope with the overflow of visitors and/or pilgrims who could not find room at the overcrowded monasteries in the city. The inns provided a daily low cost meal and alcoholic beverages were served, and by the 16th century tobacco could be bought over the bar. But whilst most inns were created as a back-up building to religious establishments, they often became resting places for cut-throats and vagabonds as well as the spiritually needy.

Around the same time the nearby Buttermarket was used as a place where medieval farmers encouraged their livestock to fight. This allegedly made the meat tastier

and more tender! This place was later to become a central shopping area open to traders throughout the city; often selling butter and dairy produce as its name indicates. This charming little square was always surrounded by shops. Today they are home to Laura Ashley, Canterbury Pottery, the Talisman and a lively public house.

Move along to Mercery Lane in medieval times and the tavern known as the Cheker of Hope was the scene of 'The Beryn's Tale' - a story once purported to have been written by Chaucer after his Canterbury classics. However, this tale is now known as part of the 'Chaucer Apocrypha', material which was not written by him at all.

The list of taverns set up by the monks and friars of the city is endless. In the Burgate area is the Dolphin pub (still serving) and the old White Bull tavern was built at the corner of the Longmarket. All these buildings constructed in medieval times now play a huge part in characterising the bustling, closed-in old-world atmosphere that makes Canterbury so unique.

As one American tourist told the author: 'I just love this English city. It's so quaint. I love the little byways and cobbled streets full of little stores and pubs. It's so old-world, somehow. And the cathedral! It's breathtaking. I tell everyone at home in New York they must see Canterbury in England.'

The reign of Henry VIII (1509-1547) is marked by his decree to disband the monasteries and become 'supreme head on earth' of the Church. It should be pointed out that this wasn't the Church of England we know today. Henry always considered himself a Catholic until the day he died but his break with the Church of Rome and the authority of the Pope was mainly caused by his wish for a divorce from Catherine of Aragon, in order for him to marry Anne Boleyn. Henry appointed Thomas Cranmer as Archbishop of Canterbury in 1533, who was instrumental in Henry obtaining his divorce.

Henry VIII was a driven man. He had also nearly run out of the money his father had left in the royal purse at the time he ascended the throne. He thought nothing of acquiring the jewels and gold that once adorned the tomb of the dead martyr, Becket.

One man who dared to challenge the King, and died for it, was Sir Thomas More who was Chancellor of England between 1529 and 1532. At one time he was one of Henry VIII's most trusted civil servants. He was a writer, politician, a lawyer and also the Speaker in the House of Commons. Although the author of 'Utopia', and seen as a free thinker, More was also a devout defender of the Catholic orthodoxy.

It was this area of his life that landed him in trouble with the monarch. More refused to help Henry to divorce Catherine of Aragon and he stuck religiously to the edicts from Rome on the matter. When he continued to refuse to swear an oath to the royal succession the King had him executed in the Tower of London on July 6, 1535.

Shortly after More's death his daughter, Margaret Roper, arrived at St Dunstan's Church in Canterbury with the head of her father. Today many tourists visit this place of worship where, allegedly, Sir Thomas's head sits in an ancient box in a vault.

A year later most small monasteries that had an income of less than £200 were suppressed, then the dissolution of the larger monasteries took place. By 1539 Canterbury's religious orders had been whittled down considerably, although a few did retain some clerical power. Many monks had been pensioned off or became parish priests.

The once all-powerful St Augustine's Abbey was handed over to the royal court and was turned into a new royal palace by Henry VIII.

If Thomas Becket was Canterbury's own Marlon Brando, then it's time to introduce another star of our city - Christopher Marlowe, or Kit Marley, or Christopher Marlin, or Kit Morley - some of the names he was recorded by during his brief life!

To retain our Hollywood theme though, we could introduce him as the city's own cross between James Dean and James Bond, for Marlowe was an enigma. He has been described as a ready wit, gauche, suave, handsome with twinkling hazel eyes, dramatic, bright, musical, something of an arriviste, supremely intelligent, well travelled and also one of Elizabeth I's many spies.

So who was the real Christopher Marlowe? We know he was born on February 26 1564, and baptised at St George's Church. He was the son of John and Katherine Marlowe, the second child of nine born to the couple. (A few weeks later one William Shakespeare was baptized at Stratford, thus creating an interesting avenue in which to focus on both men, as some scholars are wont to do).

ST AUGUSTINE'S GATE 2005 C18714k (Melody Ryall)

ANNO, DNI   ÆTATIS SVÆ 2i
1585
QVOD ME NVTRIT
ME DESTRVIT

A PUTATIVE PORTRAIT OF CHRISTOPHER MARLOWE 1585 ZZZ04340
(Reproduced by courtesy of The Parker Library, Corpus Christi College, Cambridge)

It has been documented that the Marlowes were a loud, boisterous family, who had no fears about stating their views in and around the parish of St George's in Canterbury. John Marlowe was a cobbler with a string of debts, which meant he was unable to afford to move his noisy family from the tiny home into which they were all squeezed. Christopher Marlowe's sister gained a reputation as a 'scowld' (a scold) - a woman to be avoided at all costs if one wished to avoid her malicious tongue. (The author wonders if Miss Marlowe was ever placed in the medieval ducking stool that can be seen today hanging over the river near the Weavers' House in the High Street.)

THE DUCKING STOOL c1955 C18066x

THE DUCKING STOOL 2005 C18715k (Simon Hildrew)

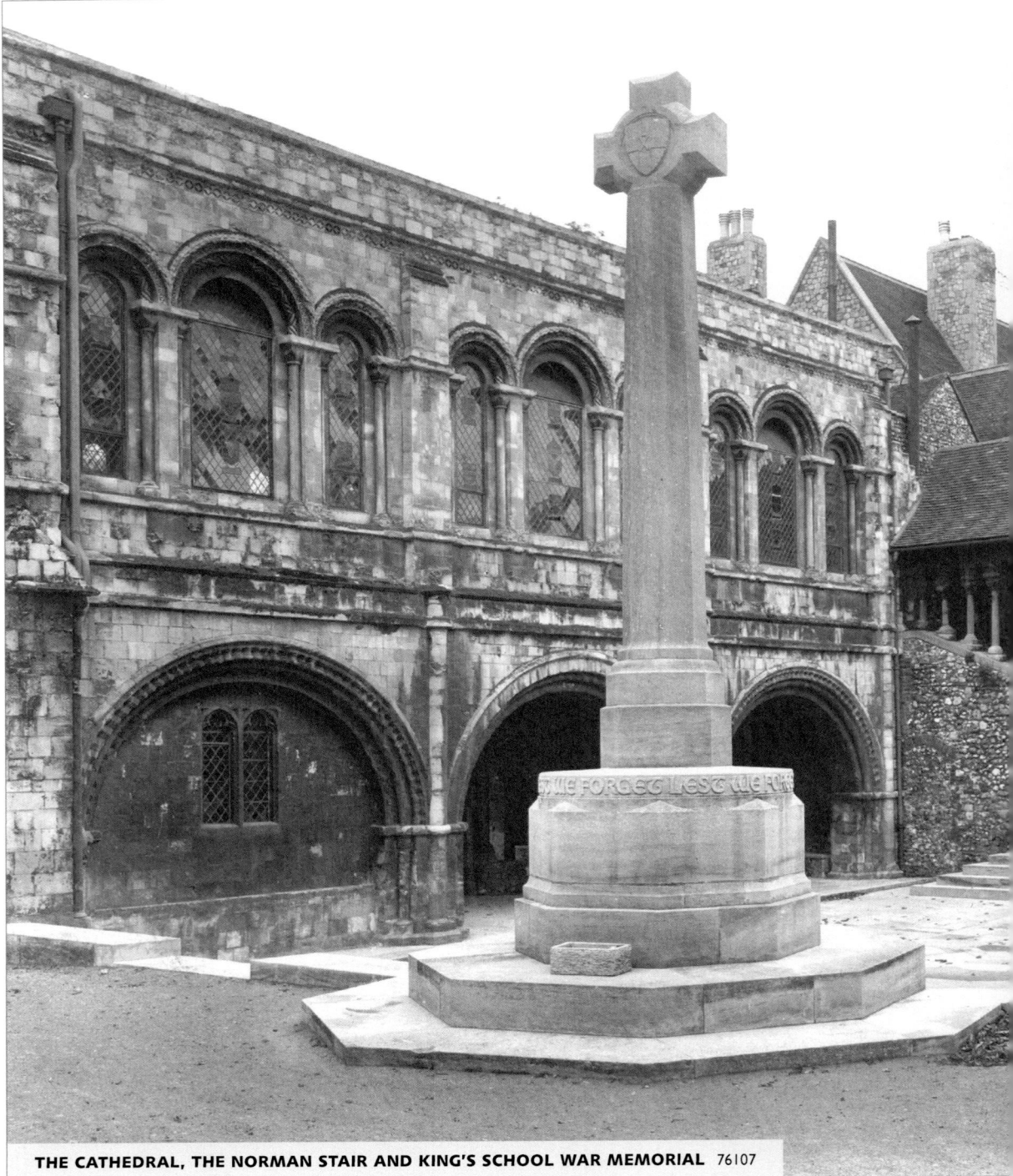

THE CATHEDRAL, THE NORMAN STAIR AND KING'S SCHOOL WAR MEMORIAL 76107

The hurly-burly Marlowe family is believed by some to have been referred to by Marlowe in a play (always attributed to Mr Shakespeare) 'The Merry Wives of Windsor'. In Act Three, scene five, a character says: 'Have I lived to be carried in a basket, like a barrow of butcher's offal?' As the Marlowes lived alongside a butcher's shop and a cattle market, this piece of dialogue could well be attributed to the young Marlowe, who would have witnessed such scenes. He also had a reputation around the city as an eavesdropper, with his keen eye always open to the main chance.

There was, though, little oubt that the cobbler's son Kit, with his cheeky retorts and clever mind, would be a ready scholar. It is documented that he was taught to read by his father and in 1568 received further education from the cathedral organist of the time, Thomas Bull. When we look at the time between his birth and his enrolment in the hallowed world of learning we discover just what a genius young Marlowe was already turning out to be. He was just four years old when Bull instructed him in the ABC, writing and Latin.

Then just before his 15th birthday, he was admitted to the King's School, founded some centuries before by King Henry II. Marlowe was accepted to the school on a special scholarship for a handful of select pupils from poor backgrounds.

At this famous school, which still remains today in the precincts of the cathedral, the city's young genius learned among many subjects, music, French, mathematics, and Italian. It was here, too, that he experienced the delights of the theatre. Records show that a good deal of money was put aside to encourage pupils to get involved in plays and performances. It was at schools like King's that travelling theatre companies tried to recruit their new protégées by promising them wealth and the chance to travel. Canterbury during those years would have also seen its fair share of players who arrived to perform miracle plays and folk-orientated entertainments. Such amusements were encouraged in 1573 when Elizabeth I swept into the city and celebrated her birthday there on 7 September 1573.

News of her arrival sent the city's elders into a flurry. Just as a royal visit today would warrant extra attention to decoration and the cleanliness of the streets, so did the announcement that Her Majesty Queen Elizabeth was on her way!

Much of the timbered effect can still be seen on the front of some of the city's buildings today. Go down Palace Street and there are some magnificent examples of Tudor and Elizabethan buildings. Over the centuries they have housed inns, antique shops and more recently an antiquarian bookshop (now sadly closed).

In the High Street there is a magnificent Elizabethan building that was once home to a popular café known as 'The Elizabethan Tearooms'. This is now closed but a sign remains to indicate that the great monarch once stayed there when she visited the city in 1573.

For the young Marlowe, though, the clock was ticking. He had spent two years at the King's School and he expressed a wish to study further and gain a Masters Degree. He chose Cambridge University's Corpus Christi College and ironically enough convinced financial benefactors, including the famous east Kent judge Roger Manwood, that he would study for seven years then enter the church. But Marlowe was telling tall stories as he was still completely fascinated by and becoming fast devoted to the idea of a life in the theatre. He wanted to take up the unusual opportunities to travel and to earn the money that the world of entertainment threw in his

Did you know?

Records of the meals Marlowe ate at Cambridge and the pennies he spent on sack and stew still exist. It is through these meticulous meal registers that historians have been able to piece together some of Marlowe's activities during his time as an undergraduate.

direction. He obviously knew deep in his heart that he would never be a bishop! This is not to say he didn't work hard.

The young writer, whose short life - like so many Elizabethans who lived on the edge - had already been packed full of rich experiences, education and adventure, began to accrue powerful friends and one particular enemy, who may have had a hand in his death.

Marlowe, ever with an eye on the political welfare of England and the royal court, made the acquaintance of Sir Francis Walsingham - the shrewd man in black who had been appointed by Elizabeth to run her intelligence operation. Walsingham was - as it were - the head of Her Majesty's MI5. It was his job to check out Catholic plots against the Protestant Queen, not only in her own country but in Europe too.

The artful, Machiavellian Walsingham was always looking for bright young men to gather information that would fuel his fervour against Catholics and traitors and young Kit Marlin (as he was known then) more than fitted the bill. Walsingham also discovered that the son of a Canterbury cobbler could also be trusted.

Within a few months Marlowe's friends noticed a change in him. His clothes were those of a dandy, with red silk linings, real gold buttons, and of the finest cut. Cambridge academics were horrified and various missives flurried around the university stating that undergraduates should only wear black or brown gowns. Attire such as that sported by the young,

suave man-about-town Marlowe was not to be encouraged! What the Cambridge academics did not realise, though, was the power of their young scholar's friends. Fairly soon any attempt to rubbish young Marlowe was immediately dismissed by the Queen's own highly regarded courtiers, and the stiff-shirted who preferred brown to red went silent.

One such emissary who sought to ruin young Kit's reputation was a spy named Richard Baines, who had been exposed in France as a poisoner by Marlowe. After this, Baines had revenge on his mind. He sought to discredit the young writer he knew took money for spying from Walsingham.

The world of espionage had taken hold of Marlowe, who had barely reached his 20s.

But as his reputation as one of the favoured among seekers of high office grew, so did evidence of his temper. Marlowe, it seems, found himself more than once thrown into jail for being involved in various fracas. He is also believed to have murdered a man during a visit to Holland and was riddled with guilt for the rest of his life, a guilt which was to become evident throughout many of the plays he wrote, especially if he was, as academic Rodney Bolt suggests, the real author of 'Hamlet' (see page 83).

He was often pardoned or released because of his powerful friends. In Elizabethan times it was believed that it was all part of a dramatist's artistic life to spend time in prison. In some quarters it was almost expected of strolling players and theatrical alchemists to do time!

The statue and statuettes outside Canterbury's Marlowe Theatre.

**THE MUSE OF LYRIC POETRY
2005** C18717k (Simon Hildrew)

**THE MUSE OF LYRIC POETRY
2005** C18716k (Simon Hildrew)

The Muse of Lyric Poetry above bronze figures of famous Victorian actors who appeared in Marlowe's plays.

**STATUE OF SIR JOHNSTON
FORBES ROBERTSON AS
DR FAUSTUS 2005**
C18718k (Simon Hildrew)

**TAMBURLAINE PLAYED BY
EDWARD ALLEYN 2005**
C18720k (Simon Hildrew)

**THE JEW OF MALTA PLAYED
BY SIR HENRY IRVING 2005**
C18722k (Simon Hildrew)

**EDWARD II PLAYED BY
JAMES K HACKETT 2005**
C18724k (Simon Hildrew)

Soon after Marlowe received his master's degree his position as a playwright was confirmed. He was the author of 'Tamburlaine' I and II; 'The Jew of Malta', 'Edward II'; 'The Tragical History of Dr Faustus'; the story poem 'Hero and Leander', and 'The Passionate Shepherd'.

It is interesting that the young writer and spy became so fixated with the devil as to pen a play about Faustus, when his time at Cambridge had been funded by a church scholarship! His play, 'The Tragical History of Dr Faustus' also reveals Marlowe's interest in magic, which obviously horrified those wrapped up in the world of Christianity!

However, despite his newfound wealth and friends, the religious and political climate in Elizabethan England was unhealthy. Elizabeth I, threatened by Mary Queen of Scots, used her spies to bring about the execution of the Scottish Queen following a series of plots made against her. Mary became involved in these plots because because she believed Elizabeth was illegitimate and that she, Mary, should sit on the throne of England. Even after she had been forced to abdicate the Scottish throne Mary foolishly took refuge in England, where she became the focus of Catholic discontent against the Protestant Queen Elizabeth.

Elizabeth's chief spy Walsingham was growing weaker. He had worked hand in glove with William Cecil, Lord Burleigh for many years. Burleigh was eventually succeeded by his son, Robert Cecil but Walsingham died in 1590. Robert Cecil became a privy councillor and then Secretary of State in 1596.

Cecil, like Baines, hated Marlowe who had been arrested a few days before his alleged death for 'heresy' and 'denying the deity of Christ'. Marlowe was freed from jail by powerful allies and when he turned up at a tavern run by one Eleanor Bull in Deptford on 30 May 1593, one of English Literature's great mysteries began.

Marlowe is generally believed to have died after a brawl over a card game, that ended with the 29-year-old dramatist dead from a stab wound above the eye. The alleged guilty party was one Ingram Frizer. However, in Rodney Bolt's fascinating book 'History Play' he suggests Marlowe did not die that night and another man was killed instead. He suggests that the young dramatist fled from Deptford, and along with a friend escaped to Vlissingen in Holland on board a ship that set sail from Gravesend. Marlowe, now exiled, then spent 16 years travelling around Europe, during which time Elizabeth I died (in 1603) and James VI of Scotland inherited the throne. To earn his keep, Marlowe joined various theatre companies and sent back plays to England via a friend. He also recruited a jobbing actor called Will Shakespeare to help put them onto the English stage.

This information is of course highly controversial if true. But Bolt is convinced that Marlowe wrote most of the works now attributed to Shakespeare. He argues Marlowe had a hugely rich and colourful life, fraught with homosexual intrigue and espionage. He was also an atheist. Much of the ingredients which made up Marlowe's extraordinary life can be witnessed in some of the plays he has had attributed to him by the pro-Marlowe scholars, especially 'King Lear' and 'Hamlet'. Shakespeare was, according to Bolt, merely a talentless chancer who passed off Marlowe's work as his own to gain reputation and wealth.

Bolt even quotes a Dr Sam Clemens who claims there is no proof to suggest Shakespeare ever wrote any plays at all. The only evidence he ever put pen to paper is in the remains of one ancient yet lowly poem.

Writer Bolt's theory is that Marlowe as a 32-year-old travelled to Italy and would have been influenced by the 'commedia dell'arte' form of improvised popular comedy. This theatrical form used stock characters like a Pedant and Harlequin. It was from his adventures in Venice and Padua that Marlowe, dazzled by new forms of theatre, became the first English dramatist to embrace the idea of character in a play instead of just the scene.

In those days there were no copyright laws so the exiled dramatist had to sit and suffer every time he heard how Shakespeare, who was becoming greedier by the day, was changing some of the lines and replacing them with laboured grammar and imagery. On top of all this, dramas were reworked by actors and other members of a theatrical troupe who believed the performance mattered more than the words. The writer's input was often

THE MARLOWE PLAQUE 2005 C18725k (Simon Hildrew)

A plaque placed near the Marlowe Theatre marking the 400th anniversary of the playwright's death. The Latin 'ut nectar ingenium' means 'such a character of talent'.

conveniently forgotten when it came to the credits in the programme.

So when did Canterbury's own dramatic genius actually die, if not in Deptford in 1593? Bolt leaves the story open, but claims that Marlowe went in Bermuda, where he was still writing at the age of 45, but he had turned his hand to the novel instead of dramatic art.

Marlowe's association with the city remains celebrated. The theatre in the Friars is named after him and in a small patch of garden to the left of the venue is a plaque placed there in 1993 to mark the fourth centenary of his alleged death in Deptford. Just in front of the theatre is a magnificent statue. This bronze, a bare-breasted female representing the Muse of lyric poetry, was first unveiled in 1891. In the 1990s it was moved from Dane John Gardens to its current position outside the theatre. It was unveiled by the actor Sir Ian McKellan and sits atop four small bronze figures of famous Victorian actors who appeared in Marlowe's plays - Sir Henry Irving, James Hackett, Edward Alleyn, and Forbes Robertson.

In the Museum of Canterbury there is an exhibition showing the arrival in the city in the 17th century of French Huguenots, and of Walloons from the region now known as Belgium, both groups having been religious refuges from the Continent. There is also a fine account of the day a Canterbury grocer, Robert Cushman, led negotiations to hire a ship, the 'Mayflower', to transport the religious and political dissenters known to history as the 'Pilgrim Fathers' to America.

Canterbury, like most other towns and cities in England, went through an extraordinary period of turbulence in the 17th century. Religious and political disputes resulted in Civil War between Charles I and Parliament. In 1647, when Christmas celebrations in Canterbury were banned by Puritan extremists, the streets were filled with Royalist rioters. People declared they were on the side of God, King Charles and Kent. In retaliation, Oliver Cromwell ordered half the city's walls to be pulled down. Only the Westgate towers remained intact because they served as a prison. King Charles I was executed in 1649, and for the following eleven years the country was under the control of Oliver Cromwell, first as a Commonwealth and then a Protectorate. In 1660 when the monarchy was restored to power, King Charles II rode through Canterbury as part of a grand celebration tour, following his return from exile in Holland.

During the 17th century building work had continued in Canterbury. The city's fortunes revived as improved transport systems and turnpike roads made Canterbury an important location on the route between London and Dover. Still standing, and a property that attracts many visitors, is the 'leaning' house in Palace Street. This timber-fronted house is known as the 'King's School shop' and is famous because it appears to be resting on the building next door. Its front door is sharply angled. Historians believe it was built by a draper called Avery Sabine to house French weavers. His initials are near the door and the small windows at the bottom of the building were there to let in the light as the weavers worked. Today it is home to a busy city art gallery and shop.

In 1620, when the grocer Cushman organised the trip on the 'Mayflower', I wonder if he realised just how many of today's Americans would return to the city looking for the birthplace of their Canterbury ancestors.

For those who wished to make their home in Canterbury, though, there were still battles of survival. For those Huguenots and Walloons who had escaped the religious persecution in their own homelands a hundred years earlier, the peace offered them along the south-east costs of Britain made settling here the best decision.

However, Canterbury elders agreed that the visitors could stay but they must abide by the rules. Attempts were made to get them to join Anglican churches. At first all new arrivals from Flanders or Holland rented properties in and around the city, which in the 17th century had a population of around 5,000.

Soon it was realised that these city settlers from overseas had many talents and gifts and they had the capacity to bring great wealth to the city. They were weavers, carpenters, bakers and potters. At the time, too great an effort was made to keep the weavers hard at it and many of them died in poverty.

The old Weavers' House in the High Street was the centre of much of their industry. It once housed hundreds of looms and the river below, near the old King's Bridge, was used in part of the cloth-making process.

Look around the city today and many of the timbered buildings used by the Huguenots and Walloons remain. This author recommends a visit to Northgate and Palace Street, the sites of much 17th century weaving activities. In the late 16th century a crypt in the western end of the cathedral was given to the Huguenots and Walloons for worship. In 1895 their place to pray was moved to the Black Prince's chancery and there, alongside a designated organ and font, it stays. There are still services in French in this part of the cathedral.

In 2005, from spring to autumn a river trip operates from the Weavers' House, which is now a busy restaurant serving à la carte and a selection of local dishes.

Although the 17th century was a time of hard work if you were a newcomer to Canterbury not all Walloons and Huguenots remained poor like the weavers. Many Huguenots became town councillors. Those new Canterbury people, who had contributed a great deal to the industry of the city, had names like Leman, Maurois and Didier. Some decided to decided to become members of the Church of England. At 28 Palace Street it is possible to see specially tailored brickwork and bay windows that had been inspired by the influence of the new French and Belgian residents of the city. It is believed this particular house belonged to Alderman Sabine.

However, these early settlers to the city would not have lived to see the arrival of the Canterbury to Whitstable railway in 1830.

It would have been their grandchildren and great-grandchildren who would experience the extraordinary sight of the tubular old steam engine puffing along the horizon between Canterbury and the fishing town of Whitstable. What the new and early Belgian and French residents of the city would have

seen, though, in 1787 was the destruction of the city gates. This meant trade vehicles could get through more easily and the city was more approachable. Only the Westgate remained as it was the city jail. Three years later in 1790 the Dane John Mound was created to mark the spot of a Norman motte and castle. It is

MERCERY LANE. 2005 C18726k (Simon Hildrew)

Did you know?

Today, the Weavers' House is a restaurant but over the centuries it has been home to many businesses, including being known as a 'house of ill repute' in the 1950s!

A CUSTOMER AT THE WEAVERS' HOUSE RESTAURANT 2005 C18728k (Simon Hildrew)

A customer enjoys a coffee in the sunshine outside the Weavers' House which once, from the 16th century, housed the many looms owned by French Huguenots.

THE WEAVERS' HOUSE 2005
C18727k (Simon Hildrew)

believed the site was once home to a Roman burial ground. At the top an obelisk was built there by an alderman called Simmons.

Back to the city's early days of transport though and it is amazing to know the old Invicta engine built by Robert Stephenson for what became known as the Crab and Winkle Line can still be seen. It is now proudly on display at the Museum of Canterbury and attracts huge interest every year from railway buffs. Its arrival coincided with the need to capitalise on local industries and, like many areas of Britain, transport became a focal point for new business, bringing income to the local purse.

In May 1830 passengers paid 9d for a 40-minute trip from Canterbury to Whitstable on a train pulled by the Invicta engine. It went about nine miles an hour after leaving its stop at North Lane in Canterbury. According to railway historians it was quite a hairy ride! What made it even more bizarre is that the engine itself was unable to climb up any sort of incline along the route: therefore great winches were installed at the top of the hills to wind it up the track! It effectively defeated the object of steam power. However it did serve some purpose transporting coal to and fro, and in its first five years of operating almost 70,000 people journeyed in its carriages.

In 1844 the old South East Railway took over the line and continued to operate it until 1953. Today visitors notice that Canterbury has two railway stations. Canterbury West is mainly visited by trains leaving Charing Cross then taking the line towards Thanet and Ashford in Kent. The West Station was opened by South Eastern Railways on February 6 1846.

In the spring of 1860 a new line to service London Victoria and for those travelling to Dover was opened by the London, Chatham and Dover Railways. This station, which is the more central in the city, was christened Canterbury East. When the old Crab and Winkle Line opened in 1830 the population of Canterbury had reached 14,000.

THE CATHEDRAL, THE CLOISTERS 1888 21361

HERALDRY ON THE CLOISTERS' ROOF 2005 C18729k (Simon Hildrew)

Eventually the city began to re-establish itself as a place of education and by 1848 two men, Coleridge and Hope, set up a missionary college on the old St Augustine's site. By the 19th century too the King's School was recognised as the place for a boy to go if his family wished him to become a member of the professional classes.

Famous former pupils who lived and breathed the King's School environment include the 17th century scientist who discovered blood circulation, William Harvey; the author Somerset Maugham, who lived with his uncle in nearby Whitstable and attended the school in 1890; and today's best-known British astronaut, Michael Foale. Sir Patrick Leigh Fermor, the travel writer made a Companion of Literature in 1991, is another old boy of King's.

THE SIDNEY COOPER GALLERY 2005
C18730k (Simon Hildrew)

In the 19th century there were also scholarships available for those wishing to find apprenticeships. There was even an orphans' school set up. It is now known as St Edmunds,

and is situated up on the hill atop Whitstable Road. This majestic school now sits next to the turning to the University of Kent.

The Victorian era as a time of great change and industrial revolution left its mark on Canterbury in many ways. Its architecture now includes new rows of terraced homes for its workers. Its well-to-do residents sported fashionable high collars and crinolines. It was also the time when one of Britain's best-known artists flourished.

Sidney Cooper was born in Canterbury, one in a family of five children. His mother had been deserted by his father when he was just five years old and she brought up her children herself, making ends meet by working as a seamstress. Her hard work and diligent childrearing paid off, as her children

Canterbury from Tonford, (detail) 1853 ©

CANTERBURY

T.S.COOPER
Pictures by the greatest Victorian cattle-painter

A collection of national importance

LEAFLET FROM THE SIDNEY COOPER GALLERY
ZZZ04119 (© Canterbury Museums, copyright reserved 2005. Reproduced by permission of the senior curator, Ken Reedie)

As a boy Cooper sat in the streets sketching. Kind benefactors allowed him to continue exploring his passion for art, and from 1833 to 1902 his paintings were on show at the Royal Academy. Sidney Cooper became an academician, and in 1848 he received a very important commission. Queen Victoria asked him to paint her a picture of a cow. In 1901 her son, Edward VII, requested Cooper paint something wonderful for the royal nursery at Sandringham. Sidney Cooper, RA, was a man of his time and became Britain's best-known artist of pastoral scenes alongside Constable. Cooper's cow scenes in particular were, and still are, hailed as genius by art critics. Cooper, however, loved his home city and set up a modern art college, donating paintings to the museum along with amazing lithographs of the cathedral.

grew up to be fine upstanding citizens. One became Mayor of Canterbury, and Sidney's artistic talent would become world famous, as many who visit his cottage and gallery near the Westgate Towers now know.

The building now known as the Royal Museum, at 18 High Street, Canterbury, was once the Beaney Institute, so named after a James Beaney who earned huge amounts of money in 1857 from a gold mine in Melbourne, Australia. Known as 'Diamond Jimmy' he had originally been funded to study medicine by Sidney Cooper's brother George and a Doctor Rigden. When Beaney died he gave £10,000 to the city to set up an institute to educate the labouring man. It is now home to the County Library and Royal Museum.

Still on the educational front, the University of Kent was founded in 1965 on a 267 acre site on St Thomas Hill in Canterbury. In that year the first of four colleges opened overlooking the cathedral. Eliot College (named after

> ## Did you know?
> One of the famous old boys of the university's drama department is the actor Alan Davies (from the television show 'Jonathan Creek'). The library on the campus, the Templeman, is named after the vice-chancellor of 1965, Dr Geoffrey Templeman. It is now home to one of the world's best collections of British theatre history books, programmes and records.

the poet T S Eliot) welcomed in the first students. It was followed in the next three years by the opening of Rutherford College, Keynes College and Darwin College. The University of Kent was designed by Lord Holford. Today it has expanded even more, and a special development built solely for the accommodation of Japanese students can been seen near the entrance just off the Whitstable Road.

CHAPTER FOUR

Bear Necessities!

IN 1898 one of literature's greatest figures decided to move to Kent. Joseph Conrad was a Polish sailor who had taught himself to read and write in English. He was in the middle of one of his most famous works, 'Heart of Darkness', when he arrived and many more classic novels were to follow.

He was born Jozef Teodor Konrad Korzeniowski in 1857 in the Ukraine, and was soon left an orphan. His parents' Polish nationalism ultimately resulted in their deaths, a nationalism hated by the Russians, who ruled that part of the country. Aged 20, the would-be writer joined the British Merchant Navy and for twenty years he sailed the high seas, gathering what we now as know a huge amount of material for the novels he would later write. In 1886 he decided to settle in England, and he married Jessie George in 1896.

Academics describe Conrad as one of 'the first English modernists'. Today they hail his work as subtle and sophisticated, but he was forced to wait until 1913 before his stories began to sell and lift him out of poverty. His novel 'Chance' secured him a regular income. His other now famous works like 'Lord Jim' and 'Nostromo' were written before 'Chance' hit the bookshelves of Edwardian England.

When in 1919 the author arrived in the village of Bishopsbourne, just outside Canterbury, to buy the Georgian house now known as Oswalds, his opinion was remote and lofty. His sons, Boris and John, who wrote books about their lives with their father, record he said this of Oswalds: 'It has no outlook, no horizon. It is a hole - for me. My wife loves it and so - I stay.

Conrad's novel, 'Heart of Darkness', is regarded as the best of all his stories. This novel is set (just like many of Christopher Marlowe's plays) in the realms of romance and mystery with the odd murder thrown in to liven up the storyline.

Marlow - the main character - travels up the dangerous Congo River and he meets a man, Kurtz, who makes him doubt the human race and its motivations. Conrad is hailed as one of the first writers of his generation to thoroughly expose civilisation as a cruel myth.

It is no place for a seafaring man. I see nothing but fields and a wall of woods.'

Today the wall of woods has disappeared, but Oswalds remains a splendid house, which still attracts many Conrad fans. It sits next to the beautiful old church of St Mary and overlooks the sort of breathtaking countryside that made Keats weep. In the Museum of Canterbury there is a whole exhibition dedicated to Conrad, who died on 3 August 1924. Visitors can see a selection of genuine artefacts from his home - all donated by his family. There is the ink pen he used, many of his books, a round oak table, family portraits and a picture showing some of the famous visitors to Oswalds, including the writer Hugh Walpole.

A magnificent Arabian dagger presented to him by his friend and admirer, the great

T E Lawrence, is also on display. Actors have recorded excerpts from the memoirs of Conrad's sons, Boris and John, and visitors can enjoy a flavour of their father's personality and his reactions to certain issues that affected his life.

Joseph Conrad is buried in Canterbury cemetery. His tomb is a regular place of pilgrimage for admirers of his work.

But as the Conrads settled down to life in Kent, the city of Canterbury was hit by two extraordinary events. In 1908 the mayor of the city, one Francis Bennett-Goldney, was accused of being involved in the theft of the Crown Jewels of Ireland. The mayor protested his innocence, yet royal orders arrived from Buckingham Palace that because of the scandal he should give up his mayoral office. What was also interesting was that a precious jewel, which had mysteriously vanished from Dublin Castle, appeared on display at the Beaney Museum Institute in Canterbury's High Street.

The mayor was a director of the place and when questions were raised this 'stolen' item was removed from view as quickly as it arrived! But Bennett-Goldney, who had a reputation by this time as being a wily old fox, was soon back on his feet. In the general election of 1910 he won the Canterbury MP's

THE FLOOD OF 1909 ZZZ04177 (Reproduced by courtesy of Kent Libraries and Archives: Canterbury Library)

seat in the House of Commons, representing the Independent Unionist Party.

Not long after the jewellery scandal involving their mayor, the people of Canterbury were forced to endure the huge flood of October 1909. Records from the time reveal how the River Stour raced in torrents through the city and houses in St Peter's Lane found their front doors under water. The city wasn't under fire from any invaders from across the Channel. This time it was Mother Nature who decided to vent her wrath upon the area. It was also the year King Edward VII died and George V took the throne.

Two years on from the floods, though, and just as many families had restored their damp homes in the city, a great heatwave beat down.

In August 1911 the temperature in Canterbury was recorded as being a tremendously hot 98°F (37°C). This heat was so extreme it remained unchallenged until 1990, when it registered an even greater degree of heat in another part of the country.

Three years later the country found itself at war with Germany. Lord Kitchener, who was living just outside Canterbury at his estate in the village of Barham, was instructed to call the then Prime Minister, Herbert Asquith. Kitchener, who had fought in India, the Sudan and the Boer War, was then offered the job of Secretary of State for War which he accepted.

Canterbury then, like the rest of the country, was thrown into the miseries of the First World War. Thousands of young men from the

THE FLOOD OF 1909 ZZZ04176 (Reproduced by courtesy of Kent Libraries and Archives: Canterbury Library)

Canterbury area who had joined the Kentish regiments - the East Kent Buffs, the Royal West Kents and even the Battalion of Kent Cyclists - lost their lives fighting for their country.

Thousands of horses were requisitioned from local industrialists and farmers. Horses were needed to pull heavy weaponry and carry officers and messengers across the war zones of France and Belgium.

Back in the fields near Canterbury in 1917, a man named Alfred Lawrence was picking potatoes. His son Arthur (now 91) recalled: 'I was just a tot at the time but my father said every time a Zeppelin came floating overhead, everyone dived for cover among the potato plants. Me included, apparently. I was shoved nose down, like the rest of the kids helping their parents in those days!'

On 15 November 1918, news arrived that the war was over. Statistics revealed that 750,000 British men had died, and in Kent the number worked out at one in ten for every town. Many of them are buried in cemeteries in France, many from Canterbury had died in Flanders, Gallipolli, Italy, India, Germany and Mesopotamia.

Within the space of two years though, Canterbury was finding its way again and its people were trying hard to look forward to a brighter future.

THE CATHEDRAL AND THE KENT WAR MEMORIAL 1924 76106

HIGH STREET 1921 70328

In 1920, as the gloom began to lift, the arrival of one of Britain's best-loved characters cheered everyone who met him - Rupert Bear. This diminutive and inquisitive little chap was invented by Canterbury artist and writer, Mary Tourtel.

Mary who grew up in Palace Street, was 45 at the time of Rupert's arrival in the 'Daily Express' newspaper. Her husband Herbert was one of the paper's esteemed night editors and encouraged his wife to submit her cartoon of 'The Little Lost Bear'.

The editor of the paper, Lord Beaverbrook, had expressed an interest in encouraging younger readers to the Express, and so Rupert was born.

Although he was reproduced on the great London presses of the day, his creator Mary was very much a Canterbury girl. Born in 1874, she was the daughter of a stained glass artist named Samuel Caldwell. She was a pupil at the Simon Langton School and the Sidney Cooper Art School.

Failing eyesight forced Mary to retire from the easel in 1935. An artist called Alfred Bestall took on the challenge of ensuring Rupert and his friends had enough adventures to keep them busy throughout the week - and in the series of annuals which hit the bookshelves every year. Mary died in 1948, aged 74. In 1980 the artist John Harrold took on the highly responsible job of keeping Rupert alive.

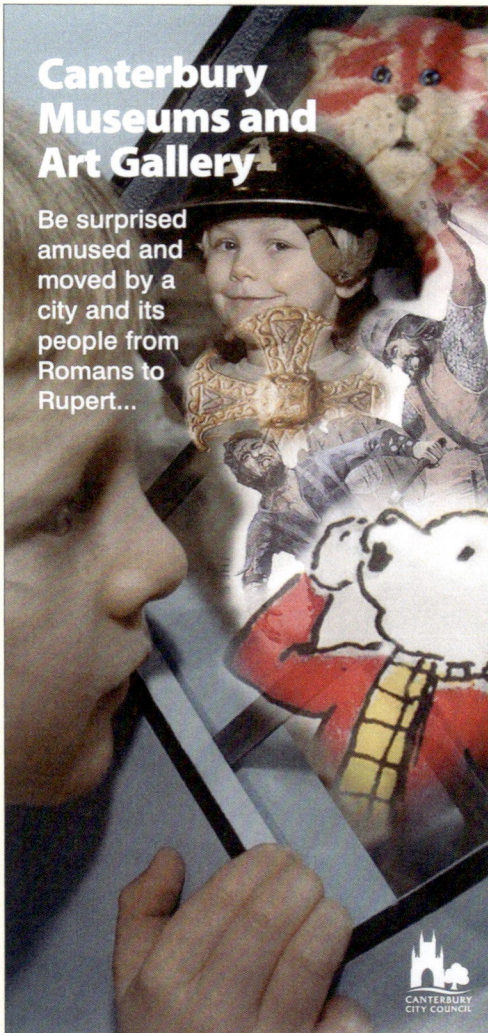

Canterbury
Museums and
Art Gallery

Be surprised
amused and
moved by a
city and its
people from
Romans to
Rupert...

CANTERBURY
CITY COUNCIL

**THE RUPERT BEAR MUSEUM IN STOUR STREET
2005** C18731k (Simon Hildrew)

Today visitors to the Museum of Canterbury, which houses the Rupert Bear Museum in Stour Street, can see rare portraits of this striking looking woman and the first-ever Rupert cartoon which appeared in the 'Daily Express' on 8 November 1920. The actual ink blotter used by Mary was recently acquired by the museum when it came up for auction.

**CANTERBURY MUSEUMS
AND ART GALLERY LEAFLET** ZZZ04139
(© Canterbury Museums, copyright reserved 2005.
Reproduced by permission of the senior curator, Ken Reedie)

In the 21st century, Rupert lives! And he still wears his classic yellow check trousers and red jumper. He remains one of the 'Daily Express's' star attractions. He also brings tens of thousands of tourists flocking to Canterbury every year.

How Mary Tourtel kept her drawings dry in 1928 is an interesting question! This was the year Canterbury was hit by a huge flood. It was caused by a great depression in the Atlantic and its effect on the city was described at the time as 'catastrophic'.

The rain just didn't stop and the city was submerged for at least a week under several feet of water which had burst out of the banks that once held the River Stour in check. Neighbours found themselves feeding each other through top windows via ladders and, as in 1909, once again rescuers relied on the horse and cart to get from one flooded street to another. Most cars were washed away: in the late 1920s they didn't have the most reliable engines.

By the mid-1930s the floods of seven years previously were only a memory. A new drama was taking place. This time T S Eliot's play, 'Murder in the Cathedral', was being staged for the first time. Based on the famous death of former Archbishop Thomas Becket, the play had seven performances at the Chapter House in the cathedral precinct and starred an east Kent actor called Robert Speaight.

In 1937, the then Archbishop of Canterbury Dr Cosmo Lang was to take part in an even bigger spectacle. It was his job to crown King George VI and Queen Elizabeth at Westminster Abbey. Two years later the men of Canterbury were being called to war again. The new Archbishop, Dean Hewlett Johnson, decided the cathedral floor must be covered with sand as a form of protection in case Hitler's bombs came crashing through the roof. Uppermost in his mind were the valuable 12th-century stained glass windows.

Decades later the great 20th-century Kent historian Bob Ogley wrote a chilling sentence in one of his many books about Kent: 'On June 2, 1942, historic Canterbury stood no longer…'

He was referring to the huge devastation inflicted on the city the day before by German bombers. Around 50 people were said to have died, 400 buildings were left in ruins and fire wrecked a further 1,500. Around the cathedral the ground was pitted out and scarred by giant trenches caused by the blast. St George's Church was described as a 'smouldering shell'. It was mostly obliterated, apart from the clock tower. The clock with its black face and gold Roman numerals was rescued by a local trader who paid for it to be repaired to full working order. The historic cathedral survived the ordeal but the stained glass windows in the nave were blown out.

The hell caused by the so-called Baedeker raids was horrific. They took place over Canterbury on May 31, June 2 and June 6 1942. These dreadful bombing attacks were named after the popular 'Baedeker' tourist guide books. Hitler decided it was the scenic and peaceful cities of England, once popular with visitors, that deserved to be destroyed, to lower British morale. Records show sixteen parachute flares fell, followed by incendiary bombs. One of these is on display at the Museum of Canterbury. Crash went the Victorian library, crash went many of the homes and shops in the High Street, Burgate, Butchery Lane, Longport, Monastery Street, St Margaret's Street and Stour Street. The anti-aircraft guns stood little chance against the swift swooping Nazi bombs that flowed from the skies. The incendiary bombs were lethal. Once they hit their targets they burst into flames, causing immediate damage and often death. The Germans dropped 6,000 on the city.

In 1942, the city was in ruins. Masonry fell in giant boulders and smashed to the ground. King's School lost part of its ancient buildings, and hundreds of firemen turned out to work around the clock to extinguish blaze after blaze after blaze. The smell of burning filled the air. Lives were in ruins and so was a once great city. Pathé newsreel shot at the time can be seen at the Museum of Canterbury, along with artefacts discovered in the ruins - a pocket watch, ration book and torn photographs of a family in happier times.

The wife of the American president, Eleanor Roosevelt, visited the city in 1942. Mrs Roosevelt met the firefighters who fought so valiantly to save the city from the flames. Interestingly enough her husband, Franklin D, came from Canterbury stock! His ancestors were the de La Noye family - some of the first Huguenots to arrive in Canterbury in the 17th century. A picture of Mrs Roosevelt looking around the bomb damage is on show at the museum.

As mentioned at the beginning of this book, it was two years after the 1942 bombing

Arthur Lawrence, who lived near the city in during the Second World War, is now 91. He recalls: 'No one could believe it, really. No one could actually take it all in for a long time. So much ruin, everywhere, and the smoke! Incredible. It choked and blackened us for weeks afterwards. The smell was awful.

'I remember walking near the cathedral at the time the Germans were dropping the incendiary bombs. The cathedral had fire wardens on the roof at the time, chucking the bombs off as they landed. We said back then if those brave souls hadn't threw them off then the cathedral would have been burned to a cinder.'

From 1939 to 1941 Arthur was requisitioned to build pillboxes - many of these small stone defences, with just a slit in the outer wall from which a soldier can aim a rifle, can be seen today in various east Kent fields and villages.

After 1941 the young builder served in the Dorsets. Today he is president of the Royal British Legion (Staple) branch. Arthur lives just outside Canterbury in the tiny village of Staple.

ARTHUR LAWRENCE 2005 C187232k (Melody Ryall)

raid that the director Michael Powell and his screenwriting colleague Emeric Pressburger shot their film 'The Canterbury Tale'.

Although he was horrified and depressed by the mess the city was in, Powell was in fact coming home to shoot his film. Born in the Canterbury village of Bekesbourne in 1905, he knew the area well.

'The Canterbury Tale', which arguably served as propaganda for the war effort, features many charming scenes that Powell no doubt recollected from his own childhood - the child talking to the GI atop a haystack, the boys' innocent games on the river. Powell once told a biographer: 'At the time nobody thought 'The Canterbury Tale' worked, but I must say it contained some of my favourite sequences.'

Although he is known for depicting a romantic outlook on life in his films, there is often a macabre twist. In 'The Canterbury Tale' he weaves in a Justice of the Peace called the Glue Man who stalks the streets at night sprinkling glue in women's hair as some sort of phallic revenge on them! Starring Eric Portman, GI Sgt John Smith and Sheila Sim, the film also featured several local boys willing to earn a shilling or two and appear on the big screen.

In 1998 Sheila Sim, wife of Sir Richard Attenborough, arrived in Canterbury to open a small exhibition in honour of 'The Canterbury Tale'. Michael Powell had died in 1990, but she met up again for the first time since 1944 with her fellow actor, the American John Smith. This author covered the event for a local newspaper and recalls how both

MICHAEL POWELL FILMING 'A CANTERBURY TALE' IN 1944 ZZZ04231 (Courtesy of the Michael Powell Estate)

MICHAEL POWELL RECEIVING HIS HONORARY DOCTORATE AT THE UNIVERSITY OF KENT IN 1984 ZZZ04230 (Courtesy of the Michael Powell Estate)

screen veterans talked happily about their wartime days filming in nearby Fordwich and Canterbury. A couple of the children who featured in the same film still lived in Canterbury in 1998, and as pensioners met the stars again - more than 50 years since, in short trousers, they'd said their goodbyes.

Also wishing the exhibition all the best and visiting the film students at Christ Church College was Thelma Schoonmaker. Known as one of Hollywood's greatest editors, Schoonmaker was married to director Powell. She received an Oscar for her work in the classic 'Raging Bull', starring Robert deNiro and directed by a huge fan of Michael Powell - one Martin Scorsese.

Powell proved to be a loyal friend to the then young Scorsese who used him as a consultant on many of his pictures in the 1970s and 1980s. It is suggested by film academics that it was Powell who made Scorsese decide to shoot 'Raging Bull' in black and white to bring out the drama and magnitude of the issues facing central character of the boxer.

Other films directed by Michael Powell include: 'The Life and Death of Colonel Blimp', 'A Matter of Life and Death', 'Black Narcissus', 'The Red Shoes', 'The Tales of Hoffman', and the controversial film 'Peeping Tom'.

But reeling back to the post-war days of 1946, the people of Canterbury celebrated a visit from King George VI, Queen Elizabeth and Princess Elizabeth. They had arrived to celebrate the remarkable survival of the cathedral. They also saw the wrecked streets of the city and the fallen masonry around the old Royal Fountain Hotel - once a favourite haunt of Queen Victoria.

Resident Arthur Lawrence recalls: 'Where all the shops had once stood before the bombing there were a lot of prefab shops, and new bridges were put up so people could walk from one side of the street to the other without falling into a gully or suchlike.'

By 1948 a new planning team had been put in place to help rebuild the city. These schemes, however, which included a new road to run in tandem with the High Street, fell on stony ground and the local council invited alternative proposals. Out of these talks came the construction of Rheims Way, which continues to serve the motorist seeking to enter or exit the city.

In 1950, with Canterbury's residents seeking relief from the struggles to survive after a world war, the old Central Cinema, hit by bomb damage, was turned into a theatre.

Three years later the Archbishop of Canterbury, Dr Geoffrey Fisher, crowned Princess Elizabeth as Queen of England at Westminster Abbey. Thousands watched the ceremony on new television sets. The people of Canterbury had seen the young queen-to-be many times. She had attended thanksgiving services at Canterbury Cathedral, and in 1949 with her new husband, Prince Philip, she honoured a service marking the 25th anniversary of the Kent Playing Fields Association.

The year 1961 marked a big day for King's School when old boy Somerset Maugham arrived to present the place with a library of his books. At the age of 49 he had become one of Britain's best-known novelists, and sales of his books, which included 'Of Human Bondage', had topped the 64 million copies mark.

HIGH STREET c1955 C18079

Kent historian and writer Bob Ogley records: 'In 1947 Maugham founded the Somerset Maugham Award, which gave young writers an opportunity to travel. On 21 September 1961 the whole of King's School was present to hear the headmaster talk of Mr Maugham's long friendship with the school: "Not content with providing us with a boathouse and physics lab, he is now giving us his books and a library. Please give him three cheers!"'

From one famous writer to another! This time in 1964 the city bid farewell to its own Ian Fleming - the man who created James Bond. Fleming was living at the nearby village of Bekesbourne when he died. He was a familiar face about Canterbury and enjoyed visiting the village pubs.

THE BOOTS SIGN 2005 C18733k (Simon Hildrew)

The old familiar Boots signs, still at the same spots 50 years later.

THE BOOTS SIGN 2005 C18734k (Simon Hildrew)

One of his favourites in particular was what is now known as the Duck, just outside the village of Bridge. Some villagers say Fleming would sit in the inn with his drink, putting together notes for the odd chapter here and there. Fleming's first book, 'Casino Royale' was published in 1953, his second book, 'Live and Let Die', came soon after, along with other great adventure stories starring the enigmatic James '007' Bond.

Fleming's novel, 'Dr No', hit the bookshelves in 1958. This was the first of his books to be turned into a blockbuster film, in 1962, which ensured him financial success. In August 1964 Fleming, who had never enjoyed robust health, died aged 56.

WESTGATE GARDENS c1955 C18043

Theatrically the city seemed to attract all the greats. By the late 1960s the Hammer Horror film star Peter Cushing had moved to nearby Whitstable with his wife, Helen. The star remained in the small fishing town until his death in 1994. His wife died in 1971. This author remembers Peter well, having as a young reporter interviewed him several times for The Kent Evening Post. He was, as everyone who knew him says, a charming man, with an honest approach to life. He was also a good painter, with a brilliant eye for stage and set design. Today, an exhibition in honour of Peter Cushing, OBE, attracts many visitors to the Whitstable Museum, about fifteen minutes' drive from Canterbury city centre.

As the 20th century drew to a close, Canterbury saw more redevelopment, both in its city centre and in the outskirts. A new hospital, the Kent and Canterbury, was built behind the flourishing home of Kent County Cricket Club (Old Dover Road). In 1980 Robert Runcie was sworn in as the new Archbishop. Seven years later in 1987, his envoy Terry Waite was kidnapped by terrorists in the Lebanon. Bundled into the back of a van, he was kidnapped and held captive by fundamentalists. There was great joy in 1991 when Terry was released, along with his fellow captive the journalist John McCarthy.

Also in 1987, a huge hurricane held Kent to ransom on 16 October. Roofs were ripped from homes, people died, cars were turned over and fences hurtled through the sky like something out of 'The Wizard of Oz'. The Meteorological Office had not predicted such a violent outbreak of storm conditions and was heavily criticised by the government. It was the famous day on which the weatherman Michael Fish failed to mention the hurricane! In not doing so, the lives of many Kent people were about to be turned upside down.

More heartbreak was on its way ten years later but it was upset of a different kind. The people of Canterbury were in mourning for Diana, the Princess of Wales. Diana was Colonel-in-Chief of the Princess of Wales' Royal Regiment, which was based in the city.

She had visited Howe Barracks several times to carry out inspections and chat to eager squaddies and their commanding officers. On 5 September 1997, a memorial service was held at which the current padre said: 'In her death we have lost not only a Colonel-in-Chief but a listener, a mother, an encourager, an ally and a supporter.'

At the cathedral the Archbishop, Dr George Carey, remembered a 'vibrant and beautiful woman who was also very vulnerable.' He went on to say: 'Out of that vulnerability came lots of strength, her passion and her commitment to people.'

In the same year the Tories came unstuck in Kent at the May general election. However Canterbury's MP, Julian Brazier, held on to his seat and continues to serve the city for another term following his successful re-election to the role in 2005.

> # Did you know?
> In 1987 a leopard escaped from John Aspinall's Howletts Zoo Park, and to this day may still be roaming the local countryside.

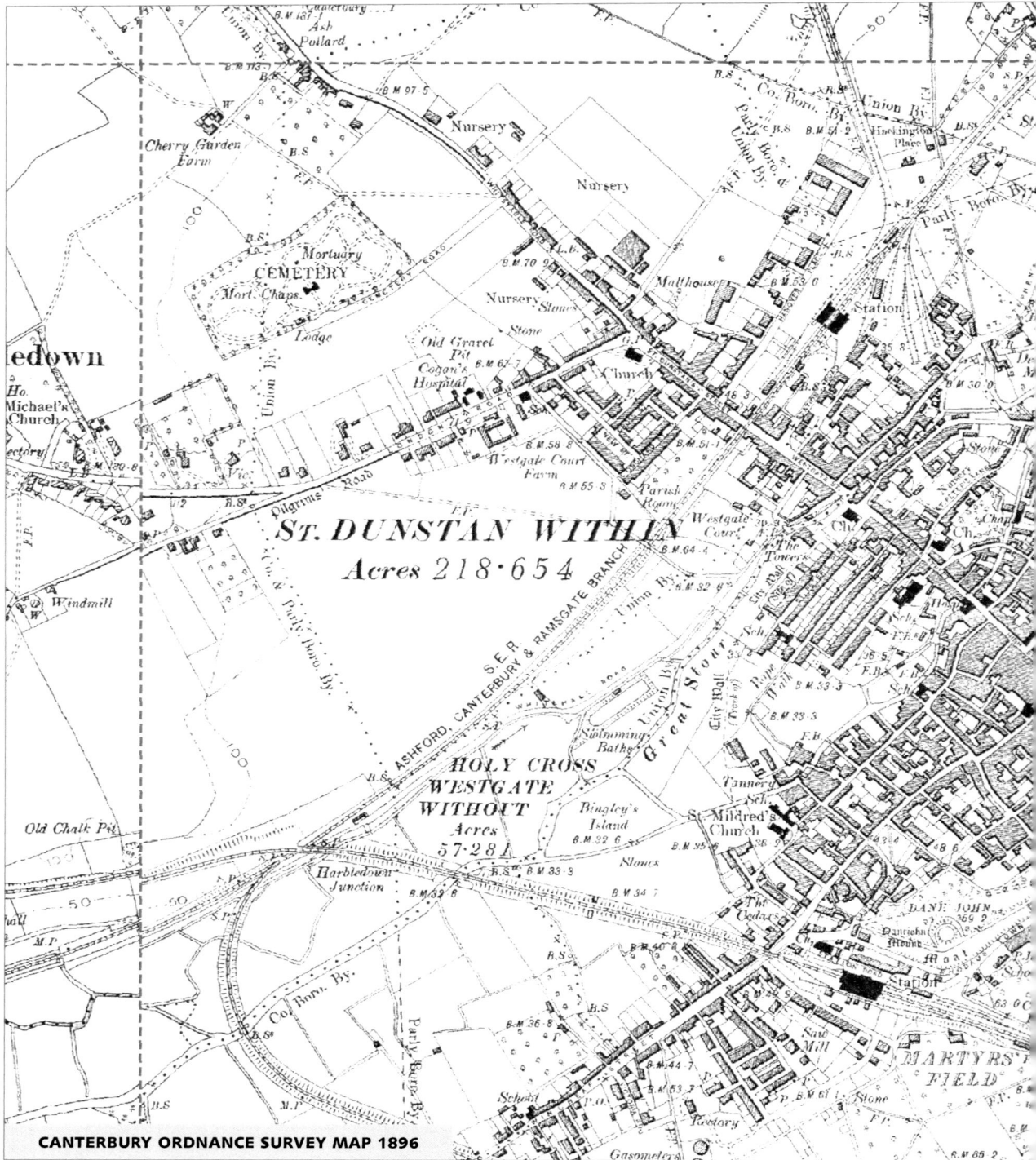

CANTERBURY ORDNANCE SURVEY MAP 1896

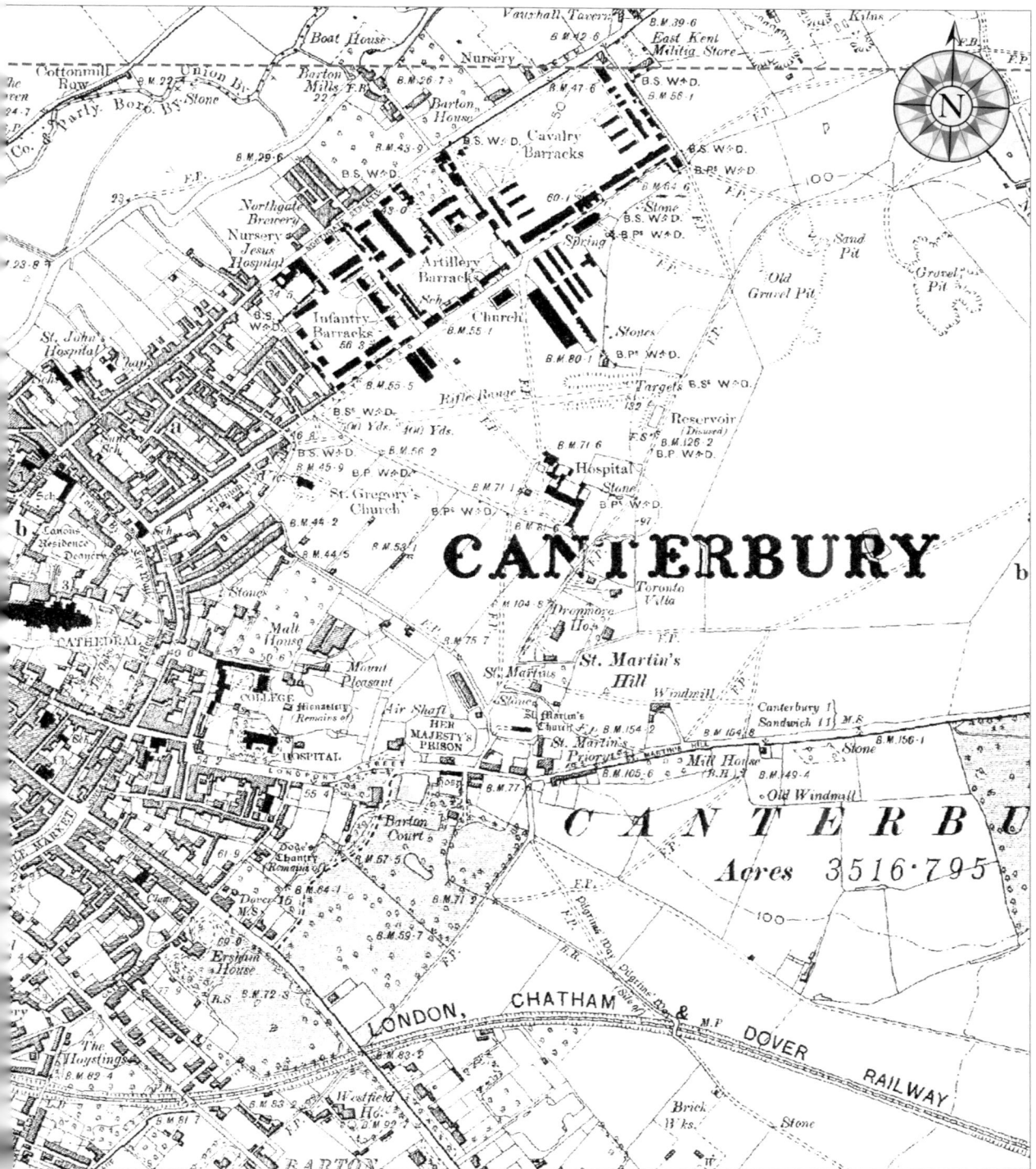

CHAPTER FIVE

Time to Celebrate

'ALL THE FRENCH GIRLS teem into the city hoping to catch sight of Mr Bloom! Alas they are rarely lucky!' says the City Museums' senior assistant curator, Martin Crowther.

So once again the city's link with the stars of today and yesteryear burns as brightly as ever. In 2005 Orlando Bloom is the city's new big hero. A star of the Hollywood blockbusting trilogy 'Lord of the Rings', Bloom was brought up in the city and his mother Sonia, a writer and businesswoman still lives in the area.

Born in 1977, from an early age the young Bloom had a passion for riding (of which he would do plenty during the making of the film of J R R Tolkien's story!). As a pupil at Canterbury's St Edmund's School he got eight O Levels and 3 A Levels and also had a chance to flex his dramatic skills.

When he was 16 he starred in National Youth Theatre productions, spent a year studying theatre in America and then in his late teens he won a place at the Guildhall School of Music and Drama. He told journalists recently that his big hero is Paul Newman. Shortly before he was due to finish his course at the Guildhall he was spotted by talent scouts as a potential cast member of director Peter Jackson's new epic, 'Lord of the Rings'.

When he was offered the part of Legolas (meaning 'green-leaf') he couldn't believe his luck. For 18 months he lived in New Zealand, learning archery, canoeing and all the skills needed to convince filmgoers he really was the character who was chosen as one of the Fellowship of the Ring.

ORLANDO BLOOM AND THELMA SCHOONMAKER
2005 ZZZ04114
(Reproduced by kind permission of Getty Images)

This photo was taken at the 77th Academy Awards ceremony on 27 February 2005. Orlando Bloom is from Canterbury, and Thelma Schoonmaker was married to Michael Powell, the famous director from Bekesbourne, near Canterbury. Thelma, a Hollywood film editor, won an Oscar for her editing of the film 'Raging Bull' starring Robert de Niro. This picture of Bloom and Schoonmaker together is quite rare – two Canterbury stars together!

Since his arrival in Hollywood, Bloom has appeared in 'Pirates of the Carribean', 'Black Hawk Down', 'The Curse of the Black Pearl', 'Troy', and Ridley Scott's 'The Kingdom of Heaven'.

What the French girls who pour into Bloom's home city know is that at the

THE MARLOWE THEATRE 2005   C18735k (Simon Hildrew)

The Marlowe Theatre in The Friars today.

moment their heart-throb remains unmarried. Emily Marseau, 17, from Bolougne, said although she came to Canterbury in the hope of seeing Bloom she wasn't too disappointed he didn't show. 'I know I was hoping too much but I love the city anyway and have been here on cross-Channel trips many times. It is a lovely city, with so much to see. The restaurants here are very good and the cathedral so 'magnifique'!'

Emily and all those who pour into its streets and alleyways are right of course. There is a lot to offer any tourist, whether they come from a neighbouring village or the other side of the world.

The city and everything it has to offer

is celebrated every year during the month-long Canterbury Festival - which started life in 1929 and is probably the oldest event of its kind in Britain.

In those days the Dean of Canterbury, George Bell, commissioned plays by eminent writers such as Laurence Binyon, Dorothy Sayers and Christopher Fry. The well-known verse drama 'Murder in the Cathedral' by T S Eliot was performed in 1935.

The great Kent actress Dame Sybil Thorndike and her husband, Lewis Casson, also took part in the festival and only the Second World War interrupted its growing success. In the 1950s a celebration, called King's Week, was set up to realise the city's potential as a cultural centre of excellence.

The committee of the Canterbury Festival kept working hard, and in 1984 a Canterbury Theatre and Festival Trust was set up. A campaign to build a new theatre was launched. This was for a venue to replace the old Marlowe Theatre, which stood in St Margaret's Street until the early 1980s when it was demolished to make way for a shopping mall now known as The Marlowe Arcade. The old Marlowe Theatre had stood on this spot for more than 50 years and at the city Local Studies Centre there is an interesting collection of theatre programmes dating back to 1967.

The city also had a Theatre Royal in the High Street dating back to 1860. Photographs and ephemera from the golden days of the city's theatrical history can also be seen at the Local Studies Centre. The Theatre Royal like the old Marlowe was replaced by the new Marlowe in 1984.

This was Canterbury City Council's cinema conversion in The Friars. Its grand opening took place that year on the first day of the Canterbury Festival. Over the years this event has grown and grown, seeing a host of famous names and faces appearing in the city's theatres, pubs, clubs, streets and galleries. Writers such as Fay Weldon, Alan Bennett, and Dr Jonathan Miller have taken part in talks, and actresses of the calibre of Dame Judi Dench have also appeared before Canterbury audiences.

TUDOR COTTAGES, BEERCART LANE 2005
C18736k (Simon Hildrew)

One of the pretty Tudor scenes in the city - this row of houses can be found in Beercart Lane.

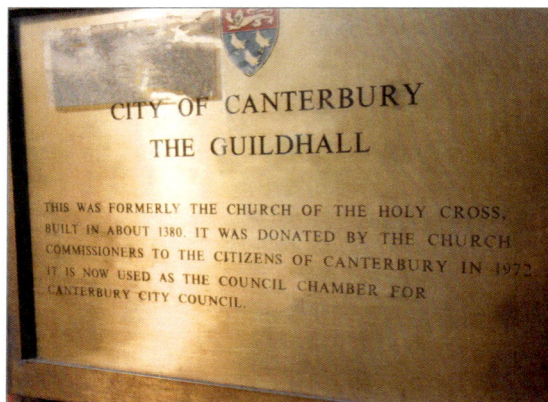

THE FORMER HOLY CROSS CHURCH IN WESTGATE GARDENS – NOW THE GUILDHALL 2005
C18737k (Simon Hildrew)

SIGN OUTSIDE THE GUILDHALL IN WESTGATE GARDENS 2005 C18738k (Simon Hildrewl)

ALONG THE RIVER 2005 C18739k (Simon Hildrew)

The two brown pillars in the middle of the picture are the only remains of an old flourmill in the city, which burned down in the 20th century. The pillars held up the old water wheel.

In 1993 thousands flocked to the city to commemorate the 400th anniversary of the death of Christopher Marlowe, and the city's Choral Society presented Marlowe's 'The Tragical History of Dr Faustus'.

A festival spokesman said that every year the events are so varied there is something for everyone, and because of this the turnover has shot up by 90% over the past six years.

For anyone arriving in Canterbury in 2001, history was on full view again too with 'The Big Dig' - an archaeological adventure in the Whitefriars area of the city. Actor and presenter Tony Robinson arrived with his 'Time Team' television crew and experts, and a wealth of artefacts were dug up. Many of these await analysis as the archaeologists focus their energies on other opportunities to uncover the city's history.

A new church now stands on the place where this dig took place and a spectacular sloping shopping mall was created, which opened in 2004 just beyond the area which had suffered so much bomb damage in the Second World War.

In April 2005 an article appeared in The Guardian's 'Review' supplement about a former King's School pupil, the travel writer Sir Patrick Leigh Fermor. In it, Sir Patrick recalled memories of his time at King's in the late 1920s - a time when he was gaining a reputation as something of a rebel - not unlike his predecessor, Christopher Marlowe.

Sir Patrick said: 'It was all rather marvellous but my discipline problems cropped up again. Things like fighting, climbing out at night, losing my books.' He told The Guardian he was often flogged for pranks and exploits and eventually expelled 'for the peccadillo of taking a walk with the daughter of a local greengrocer'.

He said: 'She was about eight years older than me - totally innocent but it was a useful pretext for the sack. Far better to get the sack for something slightly romantic than for just being a total nuisance!'

Today the city can truly claim to have everything. The phoenix that sat in the ashes caused by Hitler's bombs all those years ago, has now risen and soared high. Canterbury has, as the Dean of the cathedral, Robert Willis, said 'one of most celebrated and dedicated communities in the world'. This is a marvellous way of summing up the essence of this historic and beautiful city. It is the generations of its people who have made it the lively, thriving, mesmeric place it is today. There really is so much to enjoy and cherish in this noble and much visited city, and there is no doubt that its place on the world map is most notable.

ACKNOWLEDGEMENTS

The author would like to thank the following for their help and support during the writing of this book:

Anne Atkinson, Kate Bryson, Sara Case, Gill Cannell, Steve Crook, Martin Crowther, Simon Hildrew, Arthur Lawrence, Sarah McLeod, Bob Ogley, Michael Powell, Emeric Pressburger, Ken Reedie, Christopher Robinson, Julia Skinner, Jo Smith, Richard Thomson, Thelma Schoonmaker, Madeline and Geoff Usherwood.

BIBLIOGRAPHY

Canterbury, 2000 Years of History, Marjorie Lyle, Tempus Publishing Ltd, first published in 1994. Revised in 2002.

Drama in the Cathedral, Kenneth Pickering, Garnet Miller Publishing, 2001

Roman Canterbury, Sheppard Frere, published by A Jennings, 1965

Roman Canterbury, Andy Harmsworth & Canterbury Archaeological Trust, published by Canterbury Archaeological Trust, 1994

The Black Prince, David Cook, published by Cathedral Enterprises Ltd, 1990

Canterbury Cathedral, Jonathan Keates, published by Cathedral Enterprises Ltd, 2002

Saint Thomas Becket, Christopher Harper Bill, published by Cathedral Enterprises Ltd

In the Steps of Chaucer's Pilgrims, Jack Ravensdale, Souvenir Press, 1989

History Play, Rodney Bolt, published by Harper Collins, 2004

Francis Frith
Pioneer Victorian Photographer

Francis Frith, founder of the world-famous photographic archive, was a complex and multi-talented man. A devout Quaker and a highly successful Victorian businessman, he was philosophical by nature and pioneering in outlook. By 1855 he had already established a wholesale grocery business in Liverpool, and sold it for the astonishing sum of £200,000, which is the equivalent today of over £15,000,000. Now in his thirties, and captivated by the new science of photography, Frith set out on a series of pioneering journeys up the Nile and to the Near East.

He was the first photographer to venture beyond the sixth cataract of the Nile. Africa was still the mysterious 'Dark Continent', and Stanley and Livingstone's historic meeting was a decade into the future. The conditions for picture taking confound belief. He laboured for hours in his wicker dark-room in the sweltering heat of the desert, while the volatile chemicals fizzed dangerously in their trays. Back in London he exhibited his photographs and was 'rapturously cheered' by members of the Royal Society. His reputation as a photographer was made overnight.

By the 1870s the railways had threaded their way across the country, and Bank Holidays and half-day Saturdays had been made obligatory by Act of Parliament. All of a sudden the working man and his family were able to enjoy days out, take holidays, and see a little more of the world.

With typical business acumen, Francis Frith foresaw that these new tourists would enjoy having souvenirs to commemorate their days out. For the next thirty years he travelled the country by train and by pony and trap, producing fine photographs of seaside resorts and beauty spots that were keenly bought by millions of Victorians. These prints were painstakingly pasted into family albums and pored over during the dark nights of winter, rekindling precious memories of summer excursions. Frith's studio was soon supplying retail shops all over the country, and by 1890 F Frith & Co had become the greatest specialist photographic publishing company in the world, with over 2,000 sales outlets, and pioneered the picture postcard.

Francis Frith had died in 1898 at his villa in Cannes, his great project still growing. By 1970 the archive he created contained over a third of a million pictures showing 7,000 British towns and villages.

Frith's legacy to us today is of immense significance and value, for the magnificent archive of evocative photographs he created provides a unique record of change in the cities, towns and villages throughout Britain over a century and more. Frith and his fellow studio photographers revisited locations many times down the years to update their views, compiling for us an enthralling and colourful pageant of British life and character.

We are fortunate that Frith was dedicated to recording the minutiae of everyday life. For it is this sheer wealth of visual data, the painstaking chronicle of changes in dress, transport, street layouts, buildings, housing and landscape that captivates us so much today, offering us a powerful link with the past and with the lives of our ancestors.

Computers have now made it possible for Frith's many thousands of images to be accessed almost instantly. The archive offers every one of us an opportunity to examine the places where we and our families have lived and worked down the years. Its images, depicting our shared past, are now bringing pleasure and enlightenment to millions around the world a century and more after his death. For further information visit: www.francisfrith.co.uk

FRITH PRODUCTS & SERVICES

Francis Frith would doubtless be pleased to know that the pioneering publishing venture he started in 1860 still continues today. Over a hundred and forty years later, The Francis Frith Collection continues in the same innovative tradition and is now one of the foremost publishers of vintage photographs in the world. Some of the current activities include:

INTERIOR DECORATION

Today Frith's photographs can be seen framed and as giant wall murals in thousands of pubs, restaurants, hotels, banks, retail stores and other public buildings throughout the country. In every case they enhance the unique local atmosphere of the places they depict and provide reminders of gentler days in an increasingly busy and frenetic world.

PRODUCT PROMOTIONS

Frith products are used by many major companies to promote the sales of their own products or to reinforce their own history and heritage. Frith promotions have been used by Hovis bread, Courage beers, Scots Porage Oats, Colman's mustard, Cadbury's foods, Mellow Birds coffee, Dunhill pipe tobacco, Guinness, and Bulmer's Cider.

GENEALOGY AND FAMILY HISTORY

As the interest in family history and roots grows world-wide, more and more people are turning to Frith's photographs of Great Britain for images of the towns, villages and streets where their ancestors lived; and, of course, photographs of the churches and chapels where their ancestors were christened, married and buried are an essential part of every genealogy tree and family album.

FRITH PRODUCTS

All Frith photographs are available Framed or just as Mounted Prints and Posters (size 23 x 16 inches). These may be ordered from the address below. Other products available are - Address Books, Calendars, Jigsaws, Canvas Prints, Postcards and local and prestige books.

THE INTERNET

Already ninety thousand Frith photographs can be viewed and purchased on the internet through the Frith websites and a myriad of partner sites.

For more detailed information on Frith products, look at this site:
www.francisfrith.com

See the complete list of Frith Books at: www.francisfrith.com
This web site is regularly updated with the latest list of publications from The Francis Frith Collection. If you wish to buy books relating to another part of the country that your local bookshop does not stock, you may purchase on-line.

For further information, trade, or author enquiries please contact us at the address below:
The Francis Frith Collection, Unit 6, Oakley Business Park, Wylye Road, Dinton, Wiltshire SP3 5EU.
Tel: +44 (0)1722 716 376 Fax: +44 (0)1722 716 881 Email: sales@francisfrith.co.uk

See Frith products on the internet at www.francisfrith.com

FREE PRINT OF YOUR CHOICE

Mounted Print
Overall size 14 x 11 inches (355 x 280mm)

Choose any Frith photograph in this book.
Simply complete the Voucher opposite and return it with your remittance for £3.50 (to cover postage and handling) and we will print the photograph of your choice in SEPIA (size 11 x 8 inches) and supply it in a cream mount with a burgundy rule line (overall size 14 x 11 inches).
Please note: aerial photographs and photographs with a reference number starting with a "Z" are not Frith photographs and cannot be supplied under this offer. Offer valid for delivery to one UK address only.

PLUS: Order additional Mounted Prints at HALF PRICE - £9.50 each (normally £19.00)
If you would like to order more Frith prints from this book, possibly as gifts for friends and family, you can buy them at half price (with no additional postage and handling costs).

PLUS: Have your Mounted Prints framed
For an extra £18.00 per print you can have your mounted print(s) framed in an elegant polished wood and gilt moulding, overall size 16 x 13 inches (no additional postage and handling required).

IMPORTANT!

These special prices are only available if you use this form to order. You must use the ORIGINAL VOUCHER on this page (no copies permitted). We can only despatch to one UK address. This offer cannot be combined with any other offer.

Send completed Voucher form to:
The Francis Frith Collection, Unit 6, Oakley Business Park, Wylye Road, Dinton, Wiltshire SP3 5EU

CHOOSE A PHOTOGRAPH FROM THIS BOOK

Voucher for **FREE** and *Reduced Price Frith Prints*

Please do not photocopy this voucher. Only the original is valid, so please fill it in, cut it out and return it to us with your order.

Picture ref no	Page no	Qty	Mounted @ £9.50	Framed + £18.00	Total Cost £
		1	Free of charge*	£	£
			£9.50	£	£
			£9.50	£	£
			£9.50	£	£
			£9.50	£	£
			£9.50	£	£

Please allow 28 days for delivery. Offer available to one UK address only

* Post & handling £3.80

Total Order Cost £

Title of this book . . . .

I enclose a cheque/postal order for £ . . . . made payable to 'The Francis Frith Collection'

OR please debit my Mastercard / Visa / Maestro card, details below

Card Number:

Issue No (Maestro only):   Valid from (Maestro):

Card Security Number: Expires:

Signature:

Name Mr/Mrs/Ms . . . .

Address . . . .

. . . .

. . . .

. . . . Postcode . . . .

Daytime Tel No . . . .

Email . . . .

Valid to 31/12/12

Free Print – see overleaf

Can you help us with information about any of the Frith photographs in this book?

We are gradually compiling an historical record for each of the photographs in the Frith archive. It is always fascinating to find out the names of the people shown in the pictures, as well as insights into the shops, buildings and other features depicted.

If you recognize anyone in the photographs in this book, or if you have information not already included in the author's caption, do let us know. We would love to hear from you, and will try to publish it in future books or articles.

An Invitation from The Francis Frith Collection to Share Your Memories

The 'Share Your Memories' feature of our website allows members of the public to add personal memories relating to the places featured in our photographs, or comment on others already added. Seeing a place from your past can rekindle forgotten or long held memories. Why not visit the website, find photographs of places you know well and add YOUR story for others to read and enjoy? We would love to hear from you!

www.francisfrith.com/memories

Our production team

Frith books are produced by a small dedicated team at offices near Salisbury. Most have worked with the Frith Collection for many years. All have in common one quality: they have a passion for the Frith Collection.

Frith Books and Gifts

We have a wide range of books and gifts available on our website utilising our photographic archive, many of which can be individually personalised.

www.francisfrith.com

FF007707